READY!

Training the Search and Rescue Dog

Second Edition

By Susan Bulanda
with Larry Bulanda

i-5
PRESS

i-5 PUBLISHING, LLC™
Chief Executive Officer: Mark Harris
Chief Financial Officer: Nicole Fabian
Vice President, Chief Content Officer: June Kikuchi
General Manager, i-5 Press: Christopher Reggio
Art Director, i-5 Press: Mary Ann Kahn
Vice President, General Manager Digital: Jennifer Black
Production Director: Laurie Panaggio
Production Manager: Jessica Jaensch
Marketing Director: Lisa MacDonald

Photographs by Steve Allen, Mäike Böhm, Larry Bulanda, Susan Bulanda, Stacie Burkhardt, Terry Crooks, Beverly Fitzgerald, Elane Flower, Tracie Griego, Kevin Hoffman, Glen Holcombe, Judy Huggett, Michael Kielau, Uta Kielau, Marcia Koenig, Chris Ladoulis, Kim McKillip, Tom Orlando, Sue Purvis, Dave Rowe, Dave Salisbury, Christine Schüler, Vi Hummel-Carr Shaffer, Tammi Slater, John Strickler, and Chris Terpstra.

Illustrations by Nina Bondarenko and Tom Kimball.

Original Print ISBN: 978-159378-726-4
Copyright © 2010 Susan Bulanda   Second edition

Library of Congress Cataloging-in-Publication Data

Bulanda, Susan.
  Ready! : the training of the search and rescue dog / by Susan Bulanda with Larry Bulanda. -- 2nd ed.
     p. cm.
  Includes bibliographical references and index.
  ISBN 978-1-59378-726-4
  1. Search dogs--Training. 2. Rescue dogs--Training. I. Bulanda, Larry, 1954- II. Title.
  SF428.73.B85 2010
  636.7'0886--dc22
                              2009034444

i-5 Publishing, LLC™
3 Burroughs, Irvine, CA 92618
www.facebook.com/i5press
www.i5publishing.com

DEDICATION

To my father, whose gentleness, honesty, and love of humanity have been lifelong examples for me; and to my mother, whose love of animals has inspired me for as long as I can remember. Also to my son, Tom, who spent his entire childhood traipsing through the woods and hiding for our SAR unit and then served in Iraq with the Marines.

Equally as important, to all of the rescue people who sacrifice their time and risk their lives to save the lost and injured. So often, the press gives the canine handlers all of the attention, but they could not do their jobs without the rest of the team. These volunteers have the quiet, behind-the-scenes jobs that never make the headlines.

contents

ACKNOWLEDGMENTS

The revised edition of *READY! Training the Search and Rescue Dog* has taken as much, if not more, time and effort than did the original version, first published in 1994. I want to thank all of the people who assisted me with this edition by offering photos and information and helping me research new techniques in the field of search and rescue. I especially owe a debt of gratitude to my husband, Larry, who contributed to the writing of this second edition. He has been a SAR dog handler and incident commander for a little longer than I have. He also served on a rescue squad long before I met him.

I want to thank Vi (Hummel-Carr) Shaffer for her contributions, especially to the chapters on land cadavers and disaster dogs. Next, I want to thank Bill Dotson, who was the first person to suggest that I write this book. His faith in me gave me the courage to take on such a task at a time when few books about canine SAR existed. I want to offer a special thanks to Ken and Sharon Boyles for their confidence in me. Their concept of working with contaminated scent articles was a genuine inspiration.

I also want to thank Amy Deputato, my editor, for helping me make this edition of *READY!* an exceptional book.

INTRODUCTION

Since the first edition of this book was published, new training techniques and new search techniques have been developed, and many more units have come into operation. The use of dogs in search and rescue (SAR) has increased overall, and new jobs have become available both for dogs in general and for SAR dogs. At the same time, the growth of canine SAR units has contributed to a rise in the number of problems associated with canine SAR. In addition, there are more opinions about what constitutes a mission-ready SAR dog and what these dogs can and cannot do. In this new edition of *READY!*, I intend to clarify some of the questions that have arisen and suggest solutions to problems now being encountered. This book also includes new chapters: one about running a mission and search management, one about backtracking with a dog, and another about the politics of SAR.

Although I never intended for *READY!* to be the only resource for people who want to become SAR dog handlers and/or start a unit, the book has taken on a life of its own, has been adopted worldwide, and for many people has been the primary source of information on the subject. Therefore, I felt it was necessary to expand on my original topics in a revised edition.

This book offers the basic information about training a dog for search and rescue. When I wrote the first edition, the only similar book on the market was Sandy Bryson's *Search Dog Training*. Since that time, other books have been written that detail specialized aspects of canine SAR work. They are listed at the end of this book.

My husband, Larry, who has conducted specialized studies about canine scenting ability for Johns Hopkins University Applied Physics Laboratory and who has been an incident commander, land search manager, and rescue-squad member, has contributed to every chapter of this book.

We wish to stress that there are many right ways to train a dog. We have taken what we feel are the best of many methods—some that we've used and have worked for us and some that we've not used but have worked for others—and incorporated them into this book. We also want to stress that it takes the effort of an entire unit to teach someone to be an ethical and credible SAR dog handler; without that joint effort and dedication, the missing person's life, as well as the lives of the SAR dog and handler, could be at risk.

As you're getting started, it is essential that you understand what it means to be a SAR dog handler. The consensus among serious, professional SAR dog personnel is that a SAR dog handler is, first and foremost, a rescue person. This may mean that the SAR dog handler is certified in all of the professional training that a qualified rescue person needs to perform his job. These requirements will vary with the type of SAR work that the person will perform. Even if the type of SAR work does not require extensive rescue training, the SAR dog handler maintains the professionalism expected of a member of a rescue team at all times.

The SAR dog handler is not someone who just follows the dog through the woods. He is the other half of a team, and he must be educated in myriad subjects and employ various search strategies to conduct an effective search. It is not Lassie or Rin Tin Tin type of work; it is not a sport or a hobby. The dog is a tool that the rescue person specializes in using.

Numerous components make up a qualified K9 search unit, and the dog is just one of them. The dog is not the only resource available to the rescue person, and the dog handler will recognize and accept the fact that there are times and situations during a rescue mission where a dog is not needed. In such cases, a good SAR dog handler will be able to function in other rescue capacities, such as working on a grid team, or at least will have the professionalism and ethics to step down.

Major disasters such as 9/11 and Hurricane Katrina that have occurred since the first edition of this book was printed have given rise to widespread media coverage of the use of dogs in search and rescue. As a result, a number of well-meaning but misled people have tried to form units and train dogs. Some of those people have relied on sport-dog titles and training methods (such as those used for competitive performance events and Schutzhund) to do this. Real search and rescue work is not the same as sport-dog work, and using these methods can increase risk and liability, which can lead to the suffering or possibly the death of the missing person, the dog, the handler, and even other team members.

SAR volunteers are typically on call seven days a week, fifty-two weeks a year, including holidays. Training sessions usually are held once a week for the dog handlers and once a month for the entire unit. In addition to all of the time requirements, the volunteers must pay for their own equipment and any expenses connected with travel to and from missions.

It is the hope of the authors that this book will help the potential SAR dog person recognize the requirements of responsible SAR and inspire him to get the proper training needed to save lives. The appendices of this book list most of the types of training that a person needs to be a professional, ethical SAR dog handler. It is also essential that the potential SAR dog handler evaluate the qualifications of any unit that he wishes to join.

HOW TO USE THIS BOOK

Because each chapter has a wealth of information, we recommend that you read *READY!* from cover to cover. Even though you may not plan to train your dog to perform all of the types of SAR work covered in this book, the training concepts will enhance your work with your dog. We have covered the general topics from as many viewpoints as possible and discuss the basics of each SAR discipline, realizing that each is a specialty in and of itself and requires additional training.

Everyone has opinions about what works and what doesn't work and why something should be done one way versus another. If there are common problems associated with an aspect of SAR work or training, one or more solutions are offered. If one method does not work for you, do not hesitate to try another. Dogs and people are so varied that it is difficult to stick to one hard-and-fast rule about training. The main point to remember is that everything works some of the time, and nothing works all of the time. However, at no time will a SAR handler use fear or punishment as part of his training.

The levels of SAR training are broken down into small steps. Each level includes a goal, a target skill, and a method. Most levels also include descriptions of problems typically associated with each level, as well as a test.

At the end of the book are supplemental exercises and lessons that SAR dogs must learn, as well as additional problems that may be encountered. A training outline suggests what a SAR dog/handler team must know for the type of SAR work that they plan to do. Lastly, we've included a list of resources.

PART ONE

1

GETTING STARTED

CHAPTER 1

HISTORY OF CANINE SAR

The first documented cases of dogs used for search and rescue (SAR) come from the Mount Saint Bernard Hospice at the Great Saint Bernard Pass, the St. Gotthard Pass, and other Alpine passes. There is no record of the first time a dog was employed for search and rescue, but by researching available documents, we can learn when the concept of using dogs for search work was developed. A detailed record from 1698 does not indicate that the hospice monks were using dogs for this purpose; however, by 1800, the use of dogs for SAR had become commonplace at the hospice.

A letter written by the Father Superior of the Mount Saint Bernard Hospice to the editor of the *Illustrated Kennel News*, published in the 1910 book *War, Police, and Watch Dogs* by Major E. H. Richardson, reads:

Dear Sir,

The information which I can give about our dogs is not very extensive. As regards their origin, nothing certain is known. In 1698 they do not seem to have been used for the assistance of travelers, because a minute account written by a monk who lived at that time does not make any mention of them, although he carefully described when and how the monks and the Hospice servants went in search of travelers, to which parts of the pass they proceeded, and what was given to the victims when found to revive and comfort them; but this chronicler does not refer in any way to the dogs. And if dogs had been used at that epoch for rescue work that omission would indeed be astonishing, as that same monk actually mentions the dogs kept at the Hospice to turn the roasting-spit in the kitchen.

In 1800, however, the use of the dogs for the work of mercy had become habitual. To that period belongs the famous Barry, whose intelligence was the means of saving so many lives, and whose image, preserved by the art of the taxidermist, is in the museum at Berne.

Barry was credited with saving many lives during his lifetime. He was killed by a traveler who, stranded in a snowstorm, mistook Barry for a wolf and stabbed him. Despite his wounds, he returned to the Hospice to alert the monks of the lost person. By the time the monks rescued the man, Barry had died.

In 1817, there is another authentic record of a dog that, of his own accord, aroused the attention of the monks by his barking and restless running forward and back again. The monks followed him, and he led the way to a very desolate and abandoned hut, where they found a poor fellow who had sought shelter there from the snowstorm and was already unconscious. Since then, the dogs have frequently saved lives. When the weary travelers lose themselves in the pathless snow wilds, the dogs follow their traces and show them, so to say, to the monks or servants. But the ordinary and most important service which the dogs render us is to act as guides when, during the thick fogs, the violent storms, or in the night, the uncertain paths are quite hidden by snow. A well-trained dog hardly ever loses his way, and even when the snow lies fifty to eighty centimeters on the ground, he will follow exactly the direction of the narrow footpath, and, as the area is called up here in the mountain, the *piom*. One of our most famous dogs, who was named Drapeau, and who died in 1899, would go sometimes quite alone on to the mountain to look for travelers. He used to stop for a time at the point where they were likely to pass, and then return leisurely to the Hospice.

— *Le Prieur De L'Hospice.*

A WWI ambulance casualty dog, doing his job by taking an item from an unresponsive soldier, which he will bring to medics for help.

By 1899 in Europe, military ambulance dogs, also known as casualty dogs, were being used to search for wounded soldiers as well as for missing persons during peacetime. The British Army Corps had a military ambulance-dog program supervised by General Von Blumenthal. In his book, Major Richardson gives a good idea of how successful the military ambulance dogs were: "The report on a trial by a Prussian Jaeger Regiment states: 'The performances of the ambulance dogs exceeded all expectations. Under the most unfavorable circumstances—a broiling sun, among total strangers, in close overgrown country unknown to the dogs, an entire lack of scent except that of numerous foxes and other game, they carried out their work wonderfully.' "

Later, the writer continues:

[Ambulance dogs] carry on their backs a small parcel, marked on the outside with a red cross, and containing a length of bandage and small flasks of brandy and of water. On finding a wounded man, the dog allows him, if he is able, to unfasten the packet and make use of its contents; if he can then manage to walk, the dog leads him to where the field hospital is at work, to give him proper medical dressing; if not, the dog trots off to fetch the searchers, who it guides to the man it has found. The dogs are said to show great intelligence in their work, and may be compared to the famous dogs of St. Bernard.

War dogs also assisted medical personnel, such as nurses, in the field. The Airedale Terrier was one of Major Richardson's preferred working breeds.

It's important to note that the aforementioned dogs worked in very adverse conditions—such as the heat of the day. They also

One of Major Richardson's dogs, a British World War I messenger dog; on his collar is a tube in which messages were transported.

had to make decisions based on each find—whether to stay with the soldier and lead him to the hospital or to go get help. Keep in mind that the field hospital and searchers were rarely in the same place for long.

The dog's job was to aid the medical personnel in finding wounded soldiers on the battlefield. This meant that the dog was trained to ignore anyone who was standing, marching, or walking; the dog was to locate anyone sitting or lying down. The dog also had to differentiate between those soldiers who were alive, even if they were unconscious, and those who were dead. It clearly illustrates that dogs can be taught to do multiple complicated tasks.

Major Richardson clearly states that any dog can do SAR work, but he seemed to prefer Border Collies, other shepherd/sheepherding breeds, Airedale Terriers, and Bloodhounds. He worked his own Bloodhounds off leash, something not commonly done today.

The "alerts" that Richardson used fell into three categories. One was to have the dog return to the searchers, give a signal, and lead them back to the wounded soldier. Sometimes the signal in such an instance was an object that the dog took from the solider and brought back to the medical personnel. The second was to have the dog stay with the soldier and bark, and the third was to put the dog on a long leash and follow the dog to the wounded person. Richardson made it clear that one method was not better than another and that the wise trainer used the method that worked best for that individual dog.

According to Richardson, it took three months of intense training, six days a week, to qualify a dog for the military

This photo was originally captioned: "Major Richardson and his ambulance Bloodhound in the trenches at Melilla in the Spanish War, 1909."

program. The goals of the modern SAR dog are not much different from those of the early ambulance dogs. They have been adapted to modern situations and in some cases expanded upon.

These are perhaps two of the first dogs ever trained for SAR/ambulance work by Major Richardson, circa 1907. Note that they are Border Collies.

Many war dogs were trained in France; this is a Bouvier des Flandres from the Société Nationale du Chien.

CHAPTER 2

THE FUNCTIONS OF THE SAR DOG

nderstanding what jobs the SAR dog must do will help determine which dogs will succeed. Although the details about each type of SAR work can vary widely based on the geographic location and weather conditions in which the work is being done, the dog's job will remain the same: locate humans, give a signal to the handler, and realize that the problem is not over until the handler is next to the missing person.

Types of Search and Rescue Dogs

When most people think of tracking or trailing dogs, they think of Bloodhounds. In reality, many breeds can follow human scent successfully. What surprises many people is that there are Bloodhounds that do not have the ability to be good scent-detection dogs. The lesson is simple: a dog's ability to detect scent is ultimately based on the individual dog, not on the breed.

Border Collie Jib, an award-winning search and rescue dog trained and handled by Larry Bulanda.

The major restrictions that will prevent a dog from becoming a SAR dog are a lack of physical ability and a lack of desire to do the work. Physical features such as a short, pushed-in nose (as in the brachycephalic breeds); a long back (as in the Dachshund); or short legs/stature (as in the Bulldog) will render a dog incapable of doing SAR work. The breeds most commonly used for SAR work are hunting, herding, and working dogs. To better understand or decide which type of dog is best, consider what canine SAR work involves.

The scent-specific dog follows one particular person's scent, which is identified by the handler in the form of either a scent article or a footprint. Weather conditions, terrain, and the conditions where the person traveled will dictate how long

A scent-specific dog working on a tracking harness and lead stops to test the wind.

after the person went missing that the scent-specific dog can find/follow the scent. The scent-specific dog may not find the scent in the footprints, but rather in the general area where the person traveled or walked. Under certain conditions, the scent may not last long at all.

Typically, the scent-specific dog works on leash. However, the scent-specific dog can work off leash in the same manner as an airscenting dog if trained to do so. (See Chapter 10 for a discussion about tracking/trailing dogs.)

The airscenting dog finds any human scent in the area; the dog does not need a scent article. A well-trained dog can work an area where other people have walked, where there are other searchers, or where searchers have passed through.

The airscenting dog will put his nose where the scent is located, which can be up in the air, on the ground, or anywhere in between. Because the dog is looking for any human scent, there are no restrictions as to when or where the dog can work.

Airscenting dogs work off leash in a grid pattern as outlined by the handler. The airscenting dog can work with as many searchers in the team as needed.

Note: In cases where the authors have used "he" to refer to a dog or person, it is for literary convenience only. It is not our intention to imply that men or women, or male or female dogs, are better or worse for SAR work.

SAR TERMS

To avoid confusion, a list of SAR terms follows:

Alert—The signal that a dog gives when a person or target scent source has been located. Some people use the word *alert* to also describe the indication (see below), although the two are different.

Assistant—The person who, under the direction of the SAR dog handler/trainer, helps teach the dog how to find people (in the first edition of this book, this person was called the *victim*).

Command post—Location from which the search managers and incident commanders run the search mission.

Dog vest (also *SAR vest* or *shabrack*)—The vest that a dog wears to identify him as a SAR dog. The handler decides whether the dog will wear the vest on missions. Depending upon the situation, the vest can get caught, be hot in warm weather, get wet in rainy or cold conditions, or get very dirty. The dog's safety and comfort always comes first. The same consideration should be given regarding a collar for the dog.

Find—When the dog firsts finds the assistant/missing person.

Hasty search—A quick search of the areas where the missing person most likely could be, based on the situation. This is usually conducted while the rest of the mission is planned.

Incident commander (IC)—The person who is legally responsible for the search; this may or may not be the search manager.

Indication—A term used by some SAR people to refer to the signal that the dog gives to the handler when the dog returns to the handler on a refind. This is different from the alert, which is the signal given by the dog when he is next to the searched-for object.

Last known position or last known point (LKP) —The point at which there is evidence showing that the missing person was there, i.e., a parked car or wallet. This point can shift during the search based on new information.

Missing person—A person who is actually missing, not the assistant who helps in training.

Observer/flanker/field technician/spotter—The experienced person or mentor who goes along with the dog/handler team to set up the training exercises and instruct the handler how to train the dog and search the area. The observer also watches how the dog/handler team operates and may make suggestions. On a mission, this is the second person in the dog/handler team, which must consist of the dog, the dog handler, and a second person. Each person's job will depend on his training and skill level.

Point last seen (PLS) —The place where the missing person was last physically seen. This location may change based on new evidence.

Probability of area (POA) —A statistical determination by the search manager of the areas where the missing person is most likely to be found.

Probability of detection (POD) —The probability that the missing person is in a given area. Searchers need to determine this based on how well their sector was covered, and report this information to the command post.

Refind—When the dog finds the assistant, returns to the handler, gives the signal, and leads the handler back to the assistant.

Search manager—The person who has the overall responsibility of running the search mission; this may or may not be the incident commander.

A search dog and handler must be trained to work in the conditions of their area. Sue Purvis (RIGHT) with SAR dog Tasha and friend Kathy Tureck backpack along the Continental Divide in Colorado. Such excursions are a good way to test gear.

Types of Searches

There are seven major types of searches. Search dogs are trained for a specific type of search as well as the common environment for their geographical area. For example, a mountain wilderness search is handled differently and requires different equipment than a desert or forest wilderness search. It is critical for the safety of the dog/handler team that the handler understand the types of searches that he hopes to take part in with his dog. If the handler is in a position to replace a SAR dog or find his first SAR dog, he needs to be aware of the physical traits that the dog must have in order to search safely.

Wilderness or Large-Area Search

The wilderness search covers an area designated by the incident commander (IC or search manager/boss); the area can range in size from a fraction of an acre to hundreds of acres (1 square mile equals 640 acres). The terrain, each dog's ability, and the number of dogs available determine the size of each individual search sector on a mission. The dog/handler team must be able to work in all conditions for at least eight to ten hours.

The dog's job is to identify any human scent in the area. The search team and unit's main job is to *clear the area*, which means to determine that the lost person is not in the area as well as to find any evidence or clues related to the lost person (or determine that there are none in that area). In a wilderness search, the dog/handler team will either do a hasty search (such as roads, trails, and the like) or sweep in a grid pattern with the dog off leash to find any human scent (for example, a footprint, an article of clothing, or an airborne scent). Although the distance of the dog's sweeps is determined by the terrain, the dog must be willing to range at least 50 feet away from the handler. A dog that refuses to range and stays close to the handler will force the handler to walk twice as far. This will diminish the area that the handler can physically cover and will hinder the search effort.

It is necessary for the dog to navigate whatever obstacles he encounters, such as streams, logs, culverts, abandoned buildings, rubble or rock piles, and thick brush. If the dog finds the missing person, alive or dead, it is essential that the dog give the handler a readable signal, called an *alert*. The same is true if the dog finds evidence.

It is equally important that the dog perform a *refind* if the dog is out of the handler's sight and lead the handler directly back to the person or evidence. Some handlers train their dogs to stay by evidence or cadavers (human bodies or body parts) and give an alert by barking, whereas for a live person, the dog will return to the handler, give an indication, and lead the handler back to the missing person. (See Chapter 7.)

It is up to the handler to decide whether the dog will touch the missing person. However, no matter how the dog works, under no circumstances is the dog allowed to touch or move anything else found, especially evidence. The position

Doberman Pinscher, searching in the wilderness.

A SAR Beauceron being airlifted in a wilderness setting.

and location of the evidence is very important and can give the searcher or the police additional clues. In many cases, the police will send the evidence to a crime lab, and dog saliva on the evidence is an additional source of contamination, which restricts accurate analysis for identification.

When the dog/handler team has completed its search area, or *sector*, the handler is required to report to base, usually to the IC. The handler gives the IC a briefing about the quality of his mission, including the probability of detection (POD), scent clues, articles/evidence found, and the location(s) of the articles/evidence. The IC will pinpoint this information on a topographical map at base. Depending on how the dog/handler team worked, the handler will recommend whether the area needs to be searched again.

If the handler finds the missing person,

he must examine the body to see if the person is alive. If so, the handler must be able to administer first aid to keep the person alive and comfortable until qualified personnel arrive to transport the missing person to base. If the missing person is dead, the handler must never move the body. He will back out of the area, contact the authorities immediately, and secure the area.

Evidence or Small-Area Search

In these types of searches, dogs are used to look for evidence in criminal cases. Searches of this nature usually involve a small area in which the dog must do a "fine" or "detailed" search. This means looking carefully, sometimes sniffing every square foot of ground. If an object is found, the dog must not touch it, dig near it, or otherwise disturb the area.

After the HRD dog gives an alert, the handler may have to dig to find the scent source. The dog's intent interest in the spot further confirms that the handler is on target.

If the dog finds evidence, the handler must remove the dog from the site and then mark the area with yellow tape (if possible) to identify the location of the evidence. The handler will radio back to base and then wait for the police or whoever is in charge of collecting and evaluating the evidence to arrive on scene. At that point, the dog/handler team can report back to base.

Human-Remains Detection/ Cadaver Search

Human-remains detection (HRD) searching means looking for a body, body parts, items with decomposition on them, or bodily fluids. These things can be buried, hanging, submerged, or otherwise hidden from view. They may be wrapped—for example, in plastic bags, rags, or carpeting—or hidden in the trunk of a car. A body or body parts can be above ground and fragmented, as in the case of an explosion or plane crash. (See Chapter 15.) In the case of buried bodies, a dog can detect graves that are decades old. With additional training, HRD dogs can find the remains of people that have been burned in fires or whose bodies have been destroyed by other means. HRD searching is one of the disciplines that requires additional comprehensive training due to all of the factors involved.

The dogs work physically close to their handlers instead of ranging wide as in large-area searches. HRD searches are often conducted in the same manner as small-area searches. It is essential that the dogs do not give alerts on animal remains.

HRD searches can last for a long time, but the dogs typically work for only thirty minutes at a time, depending upon the situation. After a rest, the dogs can search again. Fine searching is exhausting to dogs, and the handlers must be able to determine that their dogs are really working and not just going through the motions because they are too tired to use their noses.

Water Body Location

Water searching involves using a dog or dogs to find a missing person who has drowned. In most cases, the dog works from a boat. In some cases, he will work from the shore. Because the current and wind will carry the scent of the missing person, the dog cannot always pinpoint exactly where the body is located. The handler must know the details of this type of search method to determine the meaning of the information that the dog gives him.

It is never a good idea to allow the dog to jump into the water. Although some dogs would love to do this, it is unsafe. The dogs will hang over the side of the boat; some may bite at the water and bark as their signal that they have found scent.

When the dog finds a scent, the handler must know how to direct the boat operator. The handler can only do this if he understands how the wind, water, and weather conditions affect the availability of the scent. This type of search-

A forest-service float plane and canoe with a Belgian Malinois SAR dog.

Working a disaster search is the same worldwide. Here, a disaster team from Holland practices how to maneuver safely on a rubble pile.

ing requires that the handler understand hydrology, air/water flow, and water dynamics to properly work the dog and determine the closest location to the scent source.

Avalanche Search

In an avalanche search, the dog works through the snow and gives an alert at the point where the scent exits the snow. The dog is required to dig immediately upon finding the scent; the act of digging is the alert. In this type of search, the handler is usually very close to the dog.

To save a life, avalanche searchers have to deploy and move very quickly. In an avalanche, a missing person must be found and dug out within fifteen to thirty minutes; the chance of survival diminishes quickly after that period.

Disaster Search: Live

Disaster searches refer to a wide variety of circumstances, covering all types of disasters. These include but are not limited to mudslides, rockslides, floods, collapsed structures, earthquakes, tornados, explosions, hurricanes, crashes or other accidents, and terrorist attacks. Most disasters will require a number of technically skilled individuals such as structural experts, hazardous-material specialists, confined-space technicians, and explosives experts, to name just a few.

There is never a guarantee that there are any survivors of a disaster, so the search could be 100 percent body recovery. The rescuers do not know until the search is over. The dogs and handlers must be able to deal with all of it, both mentally and physically.

Most of the time, this type of search requires that the dog be under strict off-leash control and be very agile. The handler must be able to direct the dog to areas in which the handler cannot be near the dog. The dog must be able to deal with the general chaos of a disaster situation and to work even if there is heavy equipment running nearby, people yelling or crying, and injured people in the area. Sometimes rescue personnel—as well as the victims of the disaster—may feel angry, hostile, or fearful, although it is not professional for rescuers to show such emotions while on a mission. Dogs can often detect these feelings. Nonetheless, the disaster dog must remain focused and calm and must continue to work in a reliable manner.

Whether a dog works in disaster situations or on rough terrain, agility is essential.

Labrador Retriever, searching debris.

Disaster Search: Mass-Fatality Recovery

Mass-fatality recovery disaster dogs must not alert on anything except bodies or body parts. These dogs will ignore blood and other bodily fluids that HRD dogs will locate. However, each handler must be able to read his dog's body language if the dog comes across a live person buried in rubble.

All disaster-trained dogs, unlike wilderness and urban-search dogs, must ignore clothing, furniture, and other items that will have human scent on them, alerting only on the actual missing person. Unlike in an avalanche or mudslide, where the dog can dig, it is not wise for a disaster dog to dig in rubble. The dog is required to give a focused alert.

The handler is responsible for determining what the dog's alert means in terms of where the missing person is actually located. For example, in certain situations, air currents in a rubble pile can cause the scent to channel away from the missing person.

CHAPTER 3

CHOOSING AND SOCIALIZING THE DOG

T he first decision a person faces when he decides to become a SAR dog handler is which dog to choose. If he has a dog, he may want to use that dog. If he does not have a dog, he is faced with selecting the right breed and choosing a good breeder to increase the odds that the dog will eventually qualify to become a SAR dog. Other people try to find dogs from shelters. Deciding which shelter dog will work, often without knowing anything about the dog's past, can be a challenge indeed! This chapter will help you understand how to pick a dog and what to look for, as well as how to socialize the dog.

Before Choosing the Dog

People who decide that they want to become involved in SAR work often have family pets that they want to use. Sometimes this works, but often it does not. Before a person makes his first contact with a SAR unit, it is wise for him to think about what will happen if

Susan Bulanda's search dog, Ch. Aixport du Moulin de Soulage ("Scout"), was the first Beauceron to be trained in the United States for SAR work. He was a Dual Champion as well as the most titled working Beauceron at the time.

his dog does not qualify as a SAR dog. As carefully as we try to pick our SAR dogs, *more dogs fail* than succeed at the training. There are many reasons for this; for example, if the dog is a hunting breed, he could be too game-driven for SAR work. A dog may have no interest in finding people, may have temperamental or physical limitations that are not obvious initially, could lack the ability to detect scent well enough for SAR work, or could lack the intelligence to retain what he's learned in SAR training to the necessary level. These are just some of the reasons why a dog will fail as a SAR dog.

If your dog does not succeed as a SAR dog, will you keep him and get another dog so you can try again? You cannot bring pet dogs along on SAR missions. Can you maintain two or more dogs and still be gone for days at a time on search missions? Will you find a good pet home for your dog and then try another dog? If you have a family, can they deal with the decision to place your dog with someone else? You may have to try SAR training with a number of dogs before you find one that works, especially if you adopt your potential SAR dog from a shelter or rescue group.

The same types of decisions apply to that time that always comes—the time when your trained SAR dog is too old to work in the field. Many SAR dog handlers cannot transition from their solid working partners to new, young dogs that they feel they cannot trust. The average volunteer time for a SAR dog handler is five years, because it is about that long until a SAR dog is no longer able to work in the field. Many handlers quit at that point. Those who do not want to give up SAR work must plan to find and start training their new dogs about two years before their old dogs' retirement. It is then not easy to leave the old dog behind when called for a search. And trust me—the old dog is most unhappy at being left out.

Choosing the Dog

The first step in canine SAR training is choosing the dog. If a potential handler already has a dog, the only way to find out if the dog will do the work is to try. Some dogs will fool potential handlers, and even trainers—an unlikely prospect may become the best SAR dog, while a seemingly prime candidate will turn out to be unmotivated or otherwise unsuitable for SAR work.

Trainers know that you can teach almost any dog to do almost anything using the correct training methods and motivation; however, it is unwise and potentially

Ness, the first Border Collie to be trained for SAR work in the United States, trained and handled by Larry Bulanda.

dangerous to force a dog to do SAR work if he does not like the work. It is essential for the dog to like the work if he is going to do a good, reliable job in adverse situations. Although certain breeds are favored as SAR dogs, and others are not, as I've mentioned, it is really a matter of the individual animal, not the breed.

A strong play or prey-chase drive is one of the first traits to look for in a potential SAR dog. Dogs that do not have strong drives usually are not suitable for this type of work. Other types of dogs that typically do not make good SAR dogs are those varieties or breeds that are bred to work independently of people, such as the livestock-guarding breeds, rather than with or for them. This is because the bond and teamwork that develops between the dog and handler is crucial to success.

Because most people love their dogs deeply and develop a special attachment to them, it is easy for a person to believe that his dog will perform effectively and cheerfully, when in reality the dog may not be good SAR material. The potential handler must remain objective about the dog. The SAR unit's training evaluator will help decide if a dog is a good SAR prospect. If you are in doubt, a qualified training evaluator from another unit can provide an unbiased second opinion. Remember, somebody's life may depend on the dog/handler team's ability to do its job.

When selecting a dog as a SAR prospect, you must consider that the average working dog will start to lose stamina

QUALITIES OF A SAR DOG

The ideal SAR dog is:

Bold

Calm

Confident

Curious in new situations and about new objects

Eager to please

Not aggressive toward people or other animals

Not overly dominant

Of a size and build to handle urban and wilderness situations

People-motivated

Scent-oriented rather than sight-oriented

Young and healthy enough to work for years

between the ages of eight and nine years. For some breeds, the dog's prime working years are earlier, ending between four and seven years of age. It can take up to two years for a dog/handler team to become qualified in just one area of search work. Clearly, then, the most logical choices for SAR work are younger dogs of breeds that have longer working lives. The shorter-lived breeds may work well, but using a dog of one of these breeds means that the handler will have to train new dogs more frequently.

Many handlers leave SAR work when their dogs retire because it is too difficult for them to train, trust, and bond with new, young dogs. A new dog never seems to work as well as the old dog. This is often because the old dog and handler have become a team, and the older dog has had years of experience.

Overall, the most successful SAR dogs fall into the working-, herding-, and sporting-dog types. This does not mean that the dog must be a purebred, as many mixed-breed dogs are very good candidates. However, the best mixed-breed SAR candidates often possess mental and physical traits similar to those of working, herding, or sporting breeds.

As the popularity of rare breeds has increased, more people have discovered that there is a wide variety of breeds from which to choose. Although some breeds are not as popular in the United States, many have been very successful in Europe since World War I as ambulance/casualty dogs and SAR dogs. Examples of some of the more uncommon yet successful breeds used in SAR are the Beauceron, Dutch Shepherd, Mudi, American Bulldog, and Braque du Bourbonnais, just to name a few.

Whatever the breed, your main consideration when selecting a dog is that he is free of genetic problems. Dogs that are from conformation (show) lines must be cautiously evaluated because they may not have the working ability to meet the demands of SAR work. Unfortunately, many breeds have lost the ability to perform the tasks that they were bred to do. Again, a dog's suitability for SAR work depends mainly on the individual dog.

Author Susan Bulanda with Border Collie Ness and Beauceron Scout.

Socialization

SAR dogs must be confident and sociable. Aggression toward people or other animals is not acceptable. The dog has to remain calm in high-stress situations, even when his handler is on an adrenaline "high." This composed, self-assured manner must be consistent in all situations in which there is unusual noise, unstable ground, and strong odors.

Proper socialization is critical to ensure that a dog will meet the demands of SAR work, and the younger the dog is socialized, the better the chances of success. The ideal age to start socialization is about eight weeks. Until the dog has had the necessary inoculations and an "OK" from the veterinarian, all socialization takes

Trossach's SAR team from Scotland. Courtesy Central Scotland Fire and Rescue.

place in the home. Basic obedience, using positive no-force methods such as clicker training, can start at this age. This training counts as part of the socialization program and helps develop the necessary bond that makes a stellar dog/handler team.

Socialization is not difficult, but it is time consuming when done correctly. When you are introducing the dog to new situations, it is important not to frighten him. How much you should do at once depends on the dog's age and temperament. One easy thing that you can do is take the dog on many errands or trips. Plan to introduce the dog to as many novel situations as possible. Some suggestions are an afternoon outing to a park, a visit to a playground, or a walk around a strip mall. The dog must learn that it is good to meet and greet strangers and accept hugs and kisses from children. This is very impor-

tant because in a search situation, the dog is often the symbol of hope to the family of the missing person. People will often walk up to the dog and, without asking, pet him and give him affection. Most SAR dogs double as therapy dogs when on a mission.

The dog must feel comfortable in country, suburban, and urban environments. In the city, the dog must be able to handle the sounds of heavy equipment, high traffic, and crowds of people. In the country, the dog must be able to ignore wildlife, farm animals, and all of the tempting odors associated with the outdoors. In fact, the dog must be familiar with the different odors associated with every environment; these include the smell of various fuels (for example, gas, diesel, and propane), electrical equipment, various vegetation, and pet and wild animals. In essence, when planning a

THE SAR DOG WILL BE ABLE TO HANDLE:

Sights and smells of the country

Boats—The dog will feel comfortable in and around all types of boats, both man- and motor-propelled.

Cliffs or other terrain that drops sharply—For safety reasons, the dog must be allowed to explore this type of terrain in a relaxed frame of mind so that there will be less chance of an accident. Remember, a dog's sense of depth perception and distance are not as good as a human's.

Crops—The dog must be accustomed to the sight and smell of crops; for example, the sight of tall cornstalks waving in a strong wind could be upsetting to a dog.

Farm equipment—The dog will be exposed to machinery such as tractors, reapers, balers, spreaders, sprayers, and any other equipment that is commonly used in your search area.

Felled trees and brush—The dog must feel comfortable working in tangles of branches and roots as well as walking on logs. He must be able to negotiate briars and brush.

Lakes, ponds, and streams—The dog has to be able to swim in and/or cross bodies of water but not be distracted by them when working.

Livestock—The dog cannot chase stock or be overly interested in the animals.

Wildlife—The dog cannot chase deer and other wildlife that may appear suddenly.

Sights and smells of the city

Aircraft—The dog needs to experience being near all types of aircraft.

Construction equipment—The dog should see and hear jackhammers, road graters, dump trucks, cranes, nail guns, portable generators, and any other equipment that he might find frightening.

Crowds of people and other animals—The dog can see many new people and other animals at an outdoor dog show. Other good places for this type of exposure are campgrounds, parks, dog parks, and parades.

Nursing homes and senior centers—The dog has to be at ease around people who use wheelchairs, walking aids, and other equipment, as well as those who behave and move erratically.

Traffic—Any city offers an opportunity to expose a dog to traffic situations. Many dog handlers do not realize that a dog who is raised in a quiet rural or suburban environment can be frightened by the noise, smells, and sights of a steady stream of traffic.

SAR dogs must be able to handle all types of situations, including varied modes of transport to and from search sites. Joan Hitchner and Piper with Kim McKillip and Skye from King County Search Dogs in Washington.

socialization program for your dog, think of the senses of sight, sound, smell, and touch, which includes different types of footing/flooring. The variables that are not in the dog's home environment are the ones that you will have to search for and travel to find.

Socialization means being inventive and using every situation that comes to mind, every opportunity that presents itself. Searchers always encounter new situations on missions, and the dog that is confident will not become frightened but will adapt.

The most important aspect of socialization is being sensible. Do not introduce the dog to situations in a way that will cause negative reactions, as this defeats the whole reason for socialization. The rule is to give the dog distance and time before taking him into the thick of things. For example, if you plan to take a dog to a construction site, start far enough away, at a distance where the dog merely notices the sounds. Play with the dog and then leave the area. The next session, begin at the distance where the dog felt safe, then move a short distance closer. Stop when the dog seems to notice the noise. Play with the dog and then leave. Repeat these steps until you are as close as you can safely be. If the dog seems to become frightened, go back to the distance where

Preparing a dog for SAR work involves teaching him how to wade through water and to swim comfortably. For dogs who enjoy it, water play with other dogs can also be a fun form of socialization.

the dog was comfortable. Understand that you may have to stay at a certain distance for a few sessions in order for the dog to feel safe. The progression depends entirely on the dog's comfort level.

Initial shyness or insecurity in a very young puppy is not ideal, but it is not a cause for alarm, either. This type of reaction means that the puppy needs socialization, the same as any other puppy. Many puppies go through a period of fear and shyness that proper handling and training will overcome. If in doubt, seek a qualified dog trainer who uses positive methods. A dog that is older than six months and is shy or fearful is a serious concern.

If the dog does not respond favorably to a few weeks of socialization or training, he is most likely not a candidate for SAR work. The unit training director, a dog trainer, or a canine behaviorist should make this determination.

Play sessions with you, other people, and other dogs are also important parts of socialization. If possible, allow the dog the opportunity to play with people of all ages, different races, and both sexes. Introductions to and play sessions with animals of other species are also a good idea. This will allow the dog to learn the parameters and rules and how to avoid potentially aggressive encounters.

CHAPTER 4

CONCEPTS OF DOG TRAINING

There are many books about how to train a dog, and most likely as many methods as there are dog trainers. An old joke says that if you have four dog trainers in a room, you have five opinions. While it is not the focus of this book to discuss dog-training methods in detail, it is important to have the basic concepts in mind when training a SAR dog. Some methods are tried-and-true, and some are not acceptable. The wise dog handler will memorize this chapter, because the concepts herein will help solve problems in the field.

Equipment

Before we discuss training concepts, we need to review training equipment. There are many different types of equipment available to train a dog. The following items work best for the SAR dog handler:

Search dogs must become comfortable with any equipment used during training and on missions.

Permanent neck collar— Choose a soft, flat collar that does not slip or choke the dog and can be left on him at all times. Some SAR vests can be anchored to this type of collar. The dog's permanent collar must have some sort of identification on it, listing the dog's name and phone numbers at which the handler can be reached. Accidents happen, and even SAR dogs can become separated from their handlers.

An adjustable martingale-type collar, such as the Premier brand collar, works well because the collar is loose so that the dog can slip out of it when not attached to a leash. If the dog is out of sight and gets caught in the brush, you want him to be able to get out of his collar. In some situations, the dogs do not wear collars at all for safety reasons.

Six-foot leash—The more flexible leashes of single thickness are best. The double-thick leashes tend to be more difficult to handle and to stuff into a backpack. Do not use a retractable leash.

Head harness—This is strictly for certain types of training, which are discussed later in this book.

Clicker—This is also mentioned later in the book. Clicker training is a great way to teach a dog. As a SAR dog handler, research this method thoroughly.

SAR vest, or shabrack—This is used to identify the dog as a SAR dog as well as to signal to the dog that it is SAR training/work time.

Note: Although there are some handlers and trainers who feel that there are specific circumstances in which a prong or electronic collar is beneficial, it is my belief that there are no reasons to use them.

About Dogs in General

As scientists and behaviorists learn more about the minds of animals in general, and of dogs in particular, they have come to realize what every dog lover has known since the beginning of time—dogs have emotions and feelings, they think, they have their own agendas, and they have opinions. They view the world as dogs, not as humans. They can communicate, obviously with other dogs but also with other species. They do not all have the same skills or levels of skills. They have likes and dislikes, and they vary in their intellectual ability and their drives. Dogs can also have emotional problems, such as phobias, obsessive-compulsive behavior, and nervous breakdowns.

Many dog handlers are not sure if a dog learns mostly as a result of his instincts or mostly by being taught. A dog's instincts will drive a dog to behave a certain way; for example, the Pointer will instinctively freeze and point when he detects a game bird. Yet the duration of the point and when to flush the game are things that are taught.

Instincts will color a dog's world. For example, if you take an Australian Shepherd into a field where there is a sheep and a rabbit, the Aussie will know that the rabbit is there but will focus on the sheep. On the other hand, if you take a Beagle into the same field, he will be aware of the sheep but will focus on the rabbit. However, all dogs learn regardless of their instincts, even though initial desires or behaviors are driven by instinct. The key is to remember that training can be very difficult if you try to teach a dog to go against his instincts.

Dogs go through developmental stages at a much more accelerated rate than humans do. Sometimes experiences or a lack of experiences can cause some of the problems associated with dogs or enhance genetic tendencies already present. In addition, it is important to understand something that science has confirmed—dogs have episodic memory. That means that dogs remember the past, can relate the past to the present, and can plan for the future. There is still debate among scientists as to whether dogs have the same level of episodic memory that humans have and whether they have a sense of time. Therefore, a dog may remember an event from the past but may not remember when or how long ago that event took place.

Scientists have also discovered that dogs are aware of their consciousness; dogs know that they are thinking and what they are thinking about. The latest discoveries have given us new insight into the mental abilities of dogs, opening up greater possibilities for their use. It also sheds new light on dogs' ability to be successfully cross-trained in more than one type of SAR work. Dogs are capable of sorting one task from another and not mixing them up.

A very important concept for dog handlers to understand is that dogs are not robots. If a dog knows various commands but has difficulty obeying, in most cases it is not because he is being disobedient, but because he has not had enough practice developing self-control. Dogs, like humans, must exercise self-control to obey a command that they would rather not obey. To understand this concept, think of the young dog who wants to run around and play with other dogs rather than stop and return to his handler, especially if the dog knows that returning to his handler means that the play session will end. Obeying in this situation takes self-control. Not complying has nothing to do with defiance, disobedience, or not knowing the command.

One of the most difficult concepts for dog handlers is to recognize that dogs learn from their mistakes. If a handler tries to micromanage his dog, he stifles the dog's creativity and prevents the dog from developing the ability to analyze the information at hand. For example, letting a dog overshoot scent and find it again will give the dog the experience he needs to solve problems in varying weather situations. If the dog handler tries to guide the dog through every step

of the problem, the dog will become dependent upon guidance from the handler and lose the ability and/or desire to think on his own. Micromanaging a dog teaches the dog that he is not to make a decision on his own.

With this information in mind, the potential SAR dog handler will consider all of the information about dogs in general and the various instincts of each breed when selecting the right dog for the job. All of these factors can also come into play when evaluating a potential SAR dog.

No matter what job the dog handler wants the potential SAR dog to do, the most important aspect of training a dog is the handler's philosophy about a dog's mind and feelings. This one major aspect will dictate how the handler trains the dog. One only has to look at how dog training has evolved in light of past and current knowledge and beliefs to see how much this influences a handler's techniques. For example, if a handler does not believe that a dog can detect three-day-old scent, he will never give the dog the opportunity to do it. This will limit the dog's ability. However, the handler who is willing to try and who allows the dog to work the problem as the dog is able gives the dog a chance to build up his skill level and experience. It's sort of a "nothing ventured, nothing gained" situation.

It is very important to realize that no matter what your philosophy is, no one will ever know for sure what goes on in the mind of a dog. After all, we do not know for sure what goes on in the minds of other

Thomas Bulanda spent his childhood traipsing through the woods and playing the missing person. He went on to enlist in the Marines, and he served in Iraq.

humans, so how can we possibly know the mind of another species? Therefore, as a wise handler, you will always keep an open mind.

One of the most important points to remember about training a dog, one that most people forget, is that a dog only knows what you show him. Dogs try very hard to understand what we want, but they can only read at face value the circumstances and activities that occur in training. We have no way to communicate concepts, deeper meanings, and intentions to a dog. However, I believe that over time a dog will develop an understanding of a concept with training

and a job to do. This is how a dog can take what he has been taught and apply it to a totally new situation. I have seen this happen many times in training and on searches.

About Training in General

Now that we've taken a look at how the dog views and approaches training, let's look at some factors that you, as the handler, need to understand about your own approach to training. A key factor in training success is a dog and handler who can communicate with and understand each other.

Age to Start

Dogs as young as eight weeks of age can start with search games and obedience. Before you start training a new pup, he should be bonded to you, settled in his new home, healthy, and adjusted to any food and water changes. Everything should be fun and games at this point in the dog's life. Often it is enough to start obedience games and leave the search work for a little bit later.

One Handler

Only one person trains and handles the SAR dog. This is because each person is an individual and handles a dog in his own way. Keep in mind that dogs have different relationships with different people. During SAR training, you and your dog will bond. Each of you learns how to "read" the other, a very important aspect in making a search successful. Without this bond, you may not trust each other. Although there are some dogs that will work with anyone behind them, a handler who does not know the dog well will not be able to read the subtle messages that the dog gives off during a search mission.

Physical Warm-Up

Before you begin any training session, give the dog a physical warm-up. It will help prevent injury to the dog and give you a chance to see if the dog is in any kind of pain. A physical warm-up after the ride to the training site will also help the dog loosen up and vent some of his excitement. Then, when training starts, the dog will be able to focus on the exercises at hand, allowing the training to be more successful.

Easy running, walking, or swimming, if conditions permit, are good for warming up—just enough exercise for the dog to let off steam without tiring him out. Be sure that the warm-up exercises are not playtime if play is the dog's reward for working. Always have clean-up material available in case the dog relieves himself in an area that is not appropriate.

Through the Dog's Eyes

Before you try to teach a dog what to do, you must clearly understand the dog's mindset. The dog never has the big picture at the start of an exercise. It is quite probable that the dog does not have even the slightest notion of what is expected. Often a training attempt will fail because you are asking the dog to do too much too soon, and the dog is very confused. You must review the details of the task and break it down into the smallest steps possible.

Remember that the dog does not have a clue what the ultimate goal is for the training session. This is especially true in the beginning of a SAR dog program. The training must be structured in such a way that the dog is shown what to do and rewarded for doing it. It is unfair to get angry or frustrated with a dog for something that he does not understand. Always evaluate the lesson to make sure that it is clearly teaching the dog. Never assume anything.

Dogs Do Not Speak English

One of the most important—and most difficult—concepts to keep in mind is that no matter how intelligent dogs may be or how sophisticated their system of communication is, they do not speak our language. Although some dogs seem to understand exactly what we say to them, they do not fully understand our words. They do make associations based on our behavior, recognize our moods, and learn that specific words go with specific behaviors. They can put together a "pic-ture" based on our words, tone of voice, and body language and can learn what will result from the things they observe. Never forget that our dogs are always watching us—that's how they learn to "psych us out" and manipulate us to get their way.

What dogs understand best are our body language, facial expressions, and tone of voice. When you have a bad day or do not have faith in your dog's ability to do the work, this often shows in your body language. The dog may react in a

A cartoon created by Bruce Ross, the author's cousin, exclusively for this edition of *Ready!*

negative manner, usually because he becomes confused. This will happen more often with a younger dog because the older dog has had more time to learn how to read us and to learn what some words mean.

Because dogs do not speak our language, our tone of voice is critical. Along with our body language, tone of voice is the main means we have for communicating with dogs. The proper tone of voice is directional and no-nonsense rather than questioning, pleading, dictatorial, hysterical, or loud. Dogs have an acute sense of hearing, so if a dog does not respond, it is not because he didn't hear you. Instead, it could be that the dog is choosing to ignore the command—a reaction to your negative attitude—or is confused about what is expected of him. Without realizing it, a handler can give his dog a mixed signal, which is often the cause of the dog's lack of response. Therefore, shouting at the dog will not solve a thing; however, teaching and showing the dog in a positive manner, breaking the exercise into its smallest steps to encourage success, will solve the problem.

Be Inventive

Do not get into a rut with your training routines or the places where you do your training. The dog is observing and piecing things together, making assumptions and forming ideas based on what he sees and experiences, and what he concludes may not be what you intend. For example, when you are practicing the *heel*

During training of any kind, you want your dog to be focused on you, attentively waiting for the next command.

exercise, if you always stop after twenty steps, the dog will assume that he must always stop after twenty steps. Furthermore, the dog can and often does associate the situation with the command. Therefore, if you only ever tell your dog to sit-stay while standing in front of him, the dog may not sit-stay if commanded to do so from behind.

Not all methods work all of the time for a dog. Different methods will work for different exercises. Do not hesitate to change methods and styles. Remember, dogs get bored, too.

Senses

The wise dog handler will keep all of the dog's senses in mind when training. All handlers are aware that dogs have a keen sense of smell. Dogs can detect one part per trillion. This equals about one gram, or a drop of scent from an eyedropper, spread over a city about the size of Philadelphia. Handlers also realize that dogs have an acute sense of hearing. Some dogs can hear a whistle up to a mile away, as demonstrated by sheepherding dogs who work the highlands of Scotland, England, and Wales.

However, most handlers are not sure about the eyesight of dogs. Dogs can see in low-light situations, detect motion, and see flickering light better than humans can, but they do not have the ability to focus as well on shapes as we can. Therefore, some shapes may appear as a blur to a dog. A dog can see at 20 feet what a human with 20/20 vision can see at 50–75 feet, making dogs nearsighted in comparison to humans.

Dogs can see color, but not the full range of color that humans can see. It is thought that dogs cannot see red or green but can see shades of yellow, gray, and blue, but this is not certain. If a dog's vision is similar to that of a person who is red/green colorblind, then the dog would see a red object as yellow and a green object as white or grayish.

Dogs have a wider field of vision than humans do. The exact range depends upon the shape of the dog's skull and the placement of his eyes, but in general a dog can see about 250 degrees whereas a human can see only 180 degrees, meaning that a dog's peripheral vision is greater than a human's. A dog's binocular vision range—the area viewed with both eyes—is much smaller than that of a human, about 100 degrees for a dog as opposed to 140 degrees for a human.

The dog's visual limitations will make it more difficult for him to judge depth and distance. Therefore, a dog needs exercises to build confidence in going through, jumping onto, and jumping over objects, as well as in jumping from one object to another. If your dog is afraid or hesitant to perform exercises that require visual accuracy, you must work with him to teach him how to handle these types of situations.

Never forget about the sense of touch. Dogs have touch pads on their skin that are sensitive to pressure. Their hair is connected to sensory nerves that allow them to feel when the hair moves. This is one way that dogs can feel their way around small places. Even though their skin has this high level of sensitivity, dogs do not seem to be as aware of slight temperature differences as people are.

Commands

A command always results in an action, either on the dog's part or on the handler's part. Either the dog obeys, or the handler teaches. You should never wait for the dog to figure out what the command means while you stand there, repeating the command. If the dog did not understand the first time, he will not understand the second time, the third time, or the fourth time. Repeating commands shows and teaches the dog that it is not necessary to respond the first time. When this happens, a handler often rationalizes his dog's lack of response to a command and thus inadvertently rewards it by allowing the dog to do what he wants or do nothing at all. This only encourages and reinforces the lack of response on the dog's part.

Never forget that dogs do not speak English! They will not recognize that "sit . . . *sit* . . . SIT!" is the same word repeated three times. The dog will think that the command is *sitsitsit* and that it is not necessary to move until the tone of voice is elevated.

It is also important for you to recognize that a dog cannot figure out what a word means by its context in a sentence. Therefore, you must never use the same word to mean different commands. Have a unique word for each response and a unique word for each variety of response desired.

Whatever command you decide to use for a behavior, it has to be consistent. It would be helpful for you to think of every command needed for regular training and SAR training and to make a list of the words and their applications so that mistakes are not made. An example of what not to do is to use *down* as the command for "lie down," then *get down* to command the dog not to jump on people as well as to mean "get off the furniture," and *go downstairs* to tell the dog to go to another level of the house. The word *down* in so many different contexts could confuse the dog.

Another common mistake that handlers (and dog owners in general) make is to use the dog's name instead of a command or with a command. For example, the dog may be doing something that the handler does not want the dog to do, and the handler will call the dog's name without a command. In these cases, the handler assumes that the dog will understand what the handler wants just from the handler's tone of voice. This places a huge burden on the dog to try to figure out what the handler expects of him.

Another example of this is when a dog owner wants his dog to come to him. Instead of calling out the *come* command, the owner calls out the dog's name. This habit is a hard one to break because we humans do it with each other. A parent will call out a child's name as a signal to come. The difference is that the child understands by the circumstances what is meant. The dog does not.

Motivation and Rewards

The key to successful dog training is motivating the dog enough so that he enjoys and wants to perform the task. A dog learns best when the task is meaningful to him. Proper motivation makes the lesson meaningful. Do not hesitate to use whatever works—it can be food, the dog's natural instinct or drive, or a special play session or other interaction with you. A properly motivated dog who loves the work will make a reliable SAR dog. Remember, someone's life may depend on it.

In obedience training or when doing search exercises, find out what your dog will work for. Food and attention are big motivators for many dogs.

Food Rewards

Although the use of food in training has gained popularity since this book was first written, some traditional trainers still do not like to use food rewards. They feel that a food-reward-trained dog will either lose his natural drive or will scavenge for discarded food. Neither is true, especially if the dog is properly trained and motivated. The basis of clicker training is to click and then give the dog a treat. In a short time, by association the click can replace the treat. This is a wonderful method for training the SAR dog.

A food reward is not the dog's meal. It is just a taste. It is something that the dog gets only during training, something whose smell causes the dog to "float on air." The treat must be so small that the dog almost cannot chew it; rather, it melts in the dog's mouth and is a tease.

As the lesson is learned and the dog's drive increases, the food reward is removed. How quickly you take away the food depends on how quickly the dog learns and how much he desires to do the exercise. Some dogs love to work so much that they do not need food rewards at all. When it's time for the dog to learn a new exercise, you can again reward the dog with treats until the goal is reached.

Food-reward training has some interesting points to consider. First, most dogs who are fearful or in pain will not respond to a food reward. If the dog will accept a treat, it means that the training conditions and the dog's mental state are good and that the dog is learning in a non-fearful, non-stressful, pain-free environment.

Two Bloodhounds, ready for a scent to follow. The breed's long ears and folds of skin help them gather scent.

Second, food will not diminish or replace the bond between the dog and handler any more than giving a child potato chips will make the child love the parent less. Last, never starve the dog or make him work for his dinner. The food reward is an extra-special treat.

Using food rewards is a tried and proven method that works very well. A study by professional dog trainer Margaret Gibbs illustrated that dogs learn more quickly and are more eager to work when the reward is food. Her study showed that food worked better than punishment techniques or hand signals.

Further support for the use of food rewards comes from researchers at the Veterans' Administration Medical Center in Sepulveda, California, who have discovered that a dog's memory is enhanced by hormones released during feeding. The implication is that if a dog is fed after a training exercise, it will enhance the dog's memory, enabling the dog to better retain what was learned in the lesson.

If food works for your dog, use it, but use it properly. Food is not a bribe; it is a reward for a job well done. An interesting article about food rewards is "Food for Thought" by Patricia Gail Burnham, which appeared in the April 1990 issue of *Pure-Bred Dogs/ American Kennel Club Gazette*.

Game-Play Reward

The game-play reward is an important aspect of SAR dog training. Most dog handlers use it to teach their dogs. This type of reward is fun for the handlers and for the dogs. The game-play reward keeps the dog and handler in a positive, upbeat frame of mind, enthusiastic about the training.

It is important to note that in some cases, a dog will not want the game-play reward during search training or on actual missions. There are dogs that are so focused on their work that they cannot play. Although rare, it does happen, and it's not because the handler neglected to try this method.

The game that will work for the dog will vary according to each dog. If the dog is a retriever, the game may be fetching or retrieving a ball. For some dogs, it is tug-of-war (which is fine to use, despite the opinions of some trainers, who feel that it encourages aggression). Some dogs may have unique games that they invented with their handlers, or special objects that they get to play with by themselves. Whatever the game or object, be sure that it is easy to do on a search mission. For example, if the dog's favorite toy is a bowling ball, it will not be practical to carry it in your backpack on a mission to reward the dog. (And, yes, I had a search dog who loved rolling bowling balls across the basement floor. Fortunately, we found another reward.)

The reward does not have to be a high-energy activity. If the dog loves to have his belly scratched, that can be the special interaction between the two of you at the end of a successful exercise. How-

ever, it is always a good idea, just as with food rewards, that the dog only gets the special game/interaction reward in training. If the dog can get it anytime, what is special about it? This does not mean that other games/interactions/objects cannot be used for regular fun at home. Training, however, has its own special reward.

Keep in mind also that the success of the game-play reward will depend in part on the bond between you and the dog. A good, strong bond will make the interaction special.

Finding that special something for the dog can be a challenge at times because dogs are so different from each other. Don't forget, they have feelings, ideas, and opinions. When a SAR-dog handler starts with a new dog, sometimes the methods that worked with the previous dog will not work with the new one.

The best way to find out what a dog likes is to watch him carefully when he plays alone. A dog will only do the things that he feels good about or feels a need to do. Often the dog's breed or type will dictate what meets his needs, driven by his instincts. For example, a hunting dog may enjoy searching through your pockets for a treat, a terrier may find that tugging an object with you is fun, and a Boxer may enjoy hitting a toy around with his front feet.

One thing you must know about the game-play reward is that a SAR training session is not the time to teach/discover/develop the reward game. The game-play reward is a reward for when the dog performs a specific behavior. If the dog has to learn what the reward is during search training, he will not associate it with the behavior that is being rewarded because he will not understand that the reward is a reward.

The game must be well established before SAR training starts. This way, as soon as the dog starts SAR training and you do the reward routine, the dog will know right away that you are pleased, and he will associate SAR training with fun things.

Who Rewards the Dog?

For SAR training, both you and the assistant (person who is hiding) can reward the dog. Most of the rewards come from you, the handler, but with some dogs and in some situations, it may be necessary to have the assistant give the dog a treat or reward.

At certain stages of training, however, only the handler rewards the dog. This is necessary so that the dog will not expect a reward from the assistant and stand there waiting for the reward instead of returning to the handler to give the alert. Once the dog returns to the handler, gives the alert/indication, and brings the handler back to the assistant, the assistant can then reward the dog if necessary.

Who rewards the dog and when to reward the dog as the dog is taught to apply the search skills will be a judgment call on the part of the handler. Each dog is different, and the wise handler will experiment to find the combination that works best.

Typically, the handler will initiate the game-play reward when the entire search exercise is finished, after the dog has found his missing person. This is a signal to the dog that the job has been completed. Keep in mind that the reward also builds the dog's motivation to do and finish the job. The wrong timing of the end-of-exercise reward can cause a dog to think that the job is finished when it is not. On the other hand, a little treat at each step of training in the very beginning can motivate a dog to solve the problem. The trick is to make the dog work longer and harder for the treat as quickly as possible.

If a dog has difficulty going in to a hidden assistant because the assistant is hidden in a way that the dog has not seen before, a well-timed treat can help the dog get over that quickly. Some dogs are by nature more cautious than others. On the other hand, if the dog starts to hang around near the assistant instead of finishing the exercise, it may be necessary for the assistant to withhold the treat. Some dogs are so good at detecting the scent of treats that the assistant may have to leave all treats at base or with the handler. Even if the assistant does not give the dog a treat, just knowing the treat is there may cause the dog to linger.

There are a few methods that have worked for dog handlers. One is to always have the dog receive the primary

It's important to use a reward that's exciting to the dog. Tasha gets her orange bumper reward.

reward from the assistant at the end of the exercise. This method can work well with dogs that are very bonded to their handlers. Such a dog will continue to try to get the handler to the assistant to get his reward, ensuring that the dog will always do the refind.

Another method is for only the handler to give the dog rewards. Again, because the dog wants the reward, he will make sure that the handler winds up next to the assistant so that he gets the reward. This method will depend on the level of training and whether or not the assistant rewards the dog when

making the initial find or only when the dog does the refind.

The last method is the handler/assistant-based reward. The reward comes from both or either, depending on what it takes to motivate the dog to complete the job.

Negative Reinforcement and Punishment

Negative reinforcement is something unpleasant and something that the dog can stop by ending the unacceptable activity. Auto manufacturers use negative reinforcement in the form of the annoying buzzer or beeping noise that will not stop until the seat belt is buckled. When we buckle our seat belt, the sound stops, thus rewarding us for doing what the manufacturer wants us to do. If the sound is annoying enough, people will buckle their seat belts right away to avoid it.

Electronic fences are an example of negative reinforcement used on dogs. If the dog goes within the danger zone, a warning beep sounds. If the dog continues, he gets an electric shock that will not stop until the dog moves back into the "safe" zone. The dog is able to avoid and/or stop the negative reinforcement.

Punishment techniques are different from negative reinforcement. Punishment happens whether or not the undesirable activity stops. Punishment is a coercive act that a handler inflicts on a dog for unwanted behavior. The coercive act often causes some degree of pain or discomfort to the dog. Although the dog stops the unwanted behavior, the handler may administer the punishment anyway to "teach the dog a lesson." In most cases, the handler cannot time the punishment properly, and the result is that the dog is punished after the offending act.

Examples of punishment are a shock from an electric collar, a piercing sound, a jerk on the leash, or a slap. Although punishment may work some of the time, it mentally damages the dog for the long term.

According to a study conducted by Robert Jones, PhD, Associate Professor of the Department of Psychology at the University of Texas at Austin, dogs who were punished showed a significant rise in the stress hormone cortisol, which can lead to the destruction of brain cells, resulting in memory loss. If the levels of cortisol are elevated frequently, it can weaken the immune system, causing illness. So not only is punishment detrimental to a dog's mental well-being but it could also result in memory loss and poor health.

The added danger of punishment is that the handler typically uses it when he is frustrated or angry. If a lesser level of punishment does not seem to work, a person usually increases the level of punishment. This can cause a dog to feel threatened to the point where biting is his only option. Most people do not recognize the signals that a dog will give when he has submitted to his handler's anger, and the handler will punish even more. It is a vicious cycle.

The SAR dog handler will find that avoiding both negative reinforcement and punishment techniques will make a dog a much better SAR dog—one that is happy and healthy. If you find that you are correcting your dog more than praising him for a good job, it is time to reexamine your training techniques because you are the one who is not doing a good job.

The Training Session

Your training sessions, or lessons, are where you will introduce the commands and exercises that your dog will need to know for basic control and for SAR work. Dogs can become bored quickly, so it's important to use your training time effectively to get the most out of each lesson.

Keep the Goal of Each Exercise in Mind

Handlers can often become sidetracked when training their dogs; they will try to teach too much too soon. This is easy to do if a dog seems to "get it" right away. While a dog may get it right away, all dogs (like people) need practice to perfect what they've learned and transfer these things from short-term to long-term memory. Typically it takes fifty to sixty repetitions for a lesson to be stored in long-term memory. However, these repetitions should not occur in one training session! Keep the goal of each exercise in mind and do not try to do too much too soon.

Larry with young Riley (Parson Russell Terrier) and retired SAR dog Gus (Border Collie), practicing obedience.

Short Lessons

Lessons should be kept short, especially in the beginning of the training program. If the dog becomes bored, tired, or stressed, the quality of learning will decrease. Remember, learning is stressful. Dogs need time out to think about what they have just done and learned. In the beginning, short ten- to fifteen-minute lessons work very well. Even these lessons are broken down into five-minute increments with a minute break in between.

There is a big difference between learning and practicing. We practice what we have learned, not the reverse. Once a dog understands the lesson, the dog can have longer practice sessions to hone and develop his skills. However, initially the goal of the exercise and how to perform it must be taught.

With very young dogs, under six months of age, it is important to keep the actual face-to-face lessons to the aforementioned five-minute formula. Each lesson consists of three five-minute mini-sessions with a one-minute break in between each mini-session. Therefore, the format is five minutes of work, one minute of rest, five minutes of work, one minute of rest, five minutes of work, and quit. This can be repeated throughout the day as the handler's schedule permits. This same formula works well for both SAR and obedience training.

Start and End Exercise

A clear signal to let the dog know that formal training is about to begin will help the dog understand what is expected of him. As the dog learns the lessons well, a *start exercise* signal will no longer be necessary. However, in the beginning, it is one way to communicate to the dog that the situation has changed from "hanging out together" to "learning mode." The signal can be different for each type of work. For example, you can use one signal for obedience training and another for SAR work. Dogs are very capable of understanding the difference. The signal can be anything that will not be taken for granted or misunderstood by the dog. This means that signals that the dog identifies independently will not work. An example of such a signal is when the dog comes running because the handler picks up his leash. The dog

BE CONSISTENT

If you keep changing the rules of the exercises, the dog will never know for sure what he should do at each training session. It helps the dog learn faster if your method of praise, tone of voice, and general handling is consistent. This means that the commands must be consistent as well. For example, do not use the command *come* one time and *here* another time.

will have no way of knowing what is in store—obedience, SAR training, or a simple walk—only that it is time to leave for some fun.

Have a search-training signal to help to get the dog in the right frame of mind as well as to raise the level of anticipation and excitement that enhances the dog's drive. Remember, as with all commands, the signal must be unique and consistent. The signal that you choose should be used only for SAR training.

An *end exercise* signal serves the same purpose as the *start exercise* signal. Consider that you and your dog are working together on a lesson. All of a sudden, you realize that it is time to quit, and you simply walk away. The dog is forced to figure out for himself what is going on. This puts the dog in a position to decide when training is over and when it is on. The dog must invent the rules that govern the situation. Will the dog's rules be consistent, reliable, or clear? Only the dog will know for sure.

By giving the dog a *free dog* signal, the dog will know that life has returned to status quo. Like the *start exercise* signal, it will eventually disappear as you and your dog learn to understand each other and the rules of engagement, but for a young dog who is learning, it will make life much clearer.

If The Dog Doesn't Get It

If the dog does not seem to understand the exercise, one of the first things you should do is pay attention to his physical condition. Sometimes a normally eager dog will stop working if he does not feel well, has pulled a muscle, or is overloaded, stressed, or otherwise having a bad day. If this is the case, do not train until the dog is better.

If the dog is physically OK and seems to be stuck on an exercise, he is likely confused about what you are trying to teach him. Go back to the level that the dog knows and start over from there. If starting over at an easier level does not work, reevaluate your training method, including looking for any hidden, unintentional signals you may be giving the dog. Often we ask our dog to do one thing with our verbal command but signal another command with our body language.

Make sure that the lesson is simple and clear. If you try to teach multiple tasks in one lesson, the dog could become overwhelmed.

If The Dog Refuses To Work

Sometimes a handler may feel that his dog knows an exercise but just does not want to do it. The handler may view this as the dog being stubborn or defiant. Typically, SAR dogs who have gotten a bit into training will not behave this way. If this happens with your dog, though, consider it a clear signal that something is not right. It is up to you to determine what that something is. The following checklist is a handy tool to review the possibilities:

1. Is the training technique clear to the dog?
2. Are you behaving in a negative manner (temper, anger, frustration)?
3. Are you using punishment or other negative methods?
4. Have you lowered your expectations, teaching the dog that less is expected of him?
5. Is the dog sick or injured?
6. Is the dog suffering from burnout because of too much training and not enough down time?
7. Has too much time elapsed since the last time the dog worked?
8. Did a negative experience occur during a previous training session to frighten the dog or cause him to lose confidence?

Dogs do not forget once they've learned something thoroughly. However, their feelings about working can change. It is up to you to be aware of this and try to prevent this from happening with your dog.

CHAPTER 5

BEFORE SAR TRAINING

M ost SAR dog handlers are anxious to start training their dogs for SAR work, but some handlers try to do too much too soon or want to skip the less exciting training. However, a successful handler learns that it is essential to lay the groundwork to ensure the dog's success.

Because dogs are very different, some of the exercises must be done on leash until your dog will obey off leash. Some dogs are so excited about training that they can be trusted at a young age off leash. It is up to you and your unit trainer to determine when it is safe to work your dog off leash.

Pre-training

Although many trainers like to wait until a dog is at least a year old before starting SAR training, the first level of SAR training is very successful with young puppies. You can play SAR games with the pup prior to formal search training to prepare him for SAR work. Keep in mind that regardless of whether SAR training starts at a young age,

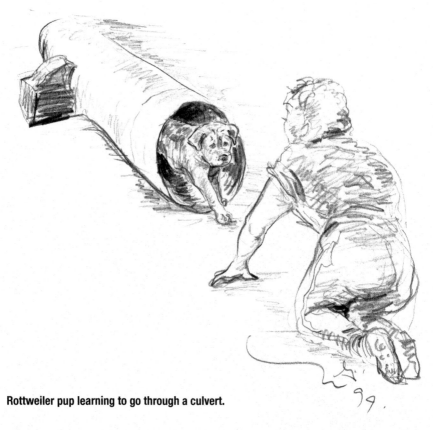

Rottweiler pup learning to go through a culvert.

the puppy is going to learn anyway. All puppies are like little sponges, so the pup may as well soak up what the handler wants him to rather than things that the handler may not want him to.

Inside the home, have the puppy search for objects, such as his toys. However, do not use any of the formal search commands that will be used later. Sit on the floor with the pup and tease him with a toy. As he gets excited about grabbing the toy, hide it on the other side of your body or under your body, making him find it. Be sure to let the puppy have the toy when he finds it. As the pup gets the idea, hide the toy around the house in easy places so the pup can find it.

Next, move the game outside to an area that is safe and secure. Never trust a pup in an open area where distractions can lure him away. If necessary, play the game with him on a long line. Because the weight of a leash can be heavy to a puppy, a length of parachute cord with a tiny clip securely fastened to his collar works very well.

For the dog who is obedient off leash, the handler can play hide-and-seek games on a hike. When you and your dog are walking in the woods, often the dog will wander ahead of you. Take these opportunities when the dog is not looking to duck behind a tree or into a bush and then call him. This will introduce a new game, and the dog will start to get the idea that the game is to find his handler. This exercise works best if the dog is bonded to you. As soon as the dog finds you, praise and make a fuss over him.

There are two benefits to this game. First, it teaches the dog to look for a person; second, it teaches the dog not to wander too far out of sight. This will not hinder the dog's ability to range in actual search training.

Dogs of any age can benefit from the pre-training games. Even seasoned SAR dogs will enjoy these games. Be careful, though, not to make the games formal training lessons. They should be all fun. Allow the dog to solve the problems or puzzles in any manner, since all dogs will use scent naturally. These games will give your dog a chance to learn how to work the wind best and will let you observe the dog's particular mannerisms as well as his natural abilities and preferences.

The wise handler will try to give the dog as many opportunities as possible to experience the conditions that he will encounter on an actual mission. This can mean letting the dog climb and walk on logs, over rock piles, or into brush; walk on a frozen lake; or do whatever else presents itself. Nevertheless, always be careful with young puppies. Jumping and climbing are to be kept to a minimum, and certain breeds that are prone to elbow and hip problems should avoid climbing and jumping as young pups. The best thing to do is talk to your veterinarian when you take your pup in for a checkup or shots. Always use common sense when exposing a dog to activities. It is important that the dog does not get injured or frightened, as this will not make SAR fun.

Keep a Record

Before starting any formal training, create a training log. The physical log must be a bound journal-type book, not a three-ring-binder, as a bound book is essential if you are ever asked to testify in court about your dog's training and ability. Keeping a journal is essential for a number of reasons:

1. It provides a record for you as well as for the unit trainer of how the dog performs and where his weaknesses and strengths are.
2. It provides a record of how the dog worked in different conditions.
3. It helps you and the trainer decide what to do to help the dog get over a slump.
4. If you have to go to court and are questioned about the dog's qualifications, the training log is proof of training and progress. No log should be only glowing reports about the dog, as this type of log can be suspect in court.

Never trust what happens during training to memory. Keep in mind that SAR dog training takes years; it is an ongoing process. No one can remember all of the details, thus your training sessions should be documented.

The training log will include, but not be limited to, the following information for each training session:

• Name of the dog
• Your name
• Date of the training session
• Weather conditions in detail—wind strength and direction, temperature, humidity level, cloud cover, and any anything else notable
• Location of training
• Terrain features
• Ground conditions
• Type of problem
• Results of the problem
• How the dog worked (such as focus, energy level, scent-detecting ability, ease of finishing the exercise)
• Manner in which the dog worked (such as his technique, how he worked the wind, how he handled obstacles)
• How you felt about the training
• How long the problem took
• Comments from the observer and/or the person who hid for the dog
• What can be done in the next training session to improve the dog and the handler

Be sure to check out the list of resources in Appendix C at the end of this book for information about a very helpful training log for SAR work by Lisa Preston: *Canine Scent Work Log*.

Obedience

There are two schools of thought about obedience in relation to SAR work. Some people feel that a SAR dog should be strictly obedience-trained while others feel that strict training hinders the dog's ability to think. It has been my experience that strict obedience has hindered many SAR dogs. After awhile, the dog will not think for himself and will wait for directions from his handler instead of working a problem out on his own. This is especially true of competitive obedience training, in which the dog is taught to wait for commands before acting.

However, as you'll see later in this book in the chapters that discuss training for the different areas of SAR, by the time you get to Level 3 of training

Lain and dog Glen of the Trossach's SAR team from Scotland.

in any discipline, you will need to have off-leash control over your dog. Some handlers use a more relaxed form of training, such as the *stay* command, to accomplish this. When given the *stay* command, the dog can stay in whatever position he sees fit, as long as he stays. In formal obedience, the *stay* would be specified as either a *sit-stay*, *down-stay*, or *stand-stay*, giving the dog no choice about how he is to stay.

The most important thing is to avoid pattern-training the dog. With pattern training, the dog learns that in certain circumstances he is to perform certain tasks. When you try to ask the dog to perform a task in a different circumstance, he may not perform the task. The dog has the concept of "I never do this there." This is detrimental for SAR work because things are never the same on actual missions.

Keep in mind that all SAR dogs must perform "intelligent disobedience." This is critical when the dog realizes that the handler has made a mistake. (Yes, handlers make mistakes all the time.) One example would be when the dog gives an alert and the handler does not believe it. The handler may feel that the missing person could not possibly be in the place that the dog is telling him. If the handler calls the dog off or tries to walk away, the dog had better insist that the handler go to the missing person, even if the dog has to grab the handler by the jacket and pull him to the missing person. This is intelligent disobedience. Guide dogs have to

do this all the time. If the blind person tells the dog to go forward and it is not safe, the dog will not go forward.

In a situation such as this, the dog faces a conflict. Obedience training dictates that the dog must come when called, but SAR trainings demands that he lead the handler to the missing person. The dog must be clear about which is most important. The only way this will happen is if the training is clear.

The best way to make things clear for the dog is to make finding the missing person the focus of the dog's training by emphasizing this through praise and rewards. In all other circumstances, the recall (*come* command) rules. Dogs are more intelligent than we previously thought, and they can make the distinction between SAR training, actual missions, and when they are off duty. During SAR work, the missing person is the priority. To help the dog understand this concept, have more SAR-training situations than obedience situations. Another way to help the dog understand the difference is to make the reward for finding the missing person much greater than the reward for obedience exercises.

Variety in training for both SAR and obedience encourages the dog to think on his own. Give the dog every opportunity to experience as many situations as possible. By working through these experiences together, you and the dog will become a team, and the dog will have a wide base of experience to draw from when new situations or problems surface.

Michael Moore (LEFT) with Shadow and David Salisbury with Flick from the UK unit, training for disaster work.

Cross-Training a Dog

A dog who is cross-trained is one who can perform in a number of SAR disciplines. This is a very debatable topic, and handlers feel strongly about both sides of the issue. Can and should the SAR dog be trained to do more than one type of searching? A cross-trained dog is very handy to have, especially if the unit is small. However, the typical handler has a limited amount of time to train the dog; therefore, a dog will usually have one primary discipline even if trained in other disciplines.

Some SAR handlers, such as human-remains detection (HRD) dog handlers, feel that their testimony in court would be invalid or severely challenged if their dogs were trained in any other type of search work. These people specialize in HRD work only.

Other people feel that a cross-trained dog will not do any of the disciplines well. However, I have very successfully cross-trained dogs to do every type of search work required for the unit's area of coverage. What is important is for the handler to recognize his dog's limitations. Not every dog can achieve the skill levels necessary to successfully operate in more than one search discipline.

If you want to cross-train a dog, it is best to start with wilderness airscent work. This teaches the dog the concept that he must find a human. The airscenting dog is free to put his nose where the scent is located rather than in a specific area only.

Dogs, by nature, are scavengers. They will look in an area for something that interests them, such as a mouse or a squirrel, and once they see something that interests them, they will focus on finding that thing. So it may be easier for a dog to grasp the concept of first looking generally (wilderness—any scent) and then narrowing down to something specific (scent-specific—a certain person).

Although the secret to cross-training a dog is simple, it does take a great deal of time. Train the dog in one discipline first. Once the dog is proficient in that type of search work and is qualified, then start another. Each type of search work must be clear to the dog. It is essential that there are different commands and different circumstances for each; be sure not to blend the two. Do not do a wilderness problem in the morning and then a disaster problem in the afternoon. Dogs who are well trained in both areas can switch, but not a dog that is learning. You must gain the knowledge and understanding of cross-training, and the dog must be proficient before you attempt to use him in the field.

Your Helpers in Training

No dog/handler team should undertake SAR training alone. It is essential that the SAR dog handler have trained rescue personnel who are experienced in SAR dog training to help. Search and rescue is a team effort, and without the support of a SAR unit, the handler cannot set up training to simulate real mission scenarios. Most units have experienced people to guide new SAR dog/handler teams.

The Assistant

The assistant, who pretends to be the missing person, is a key player who can make the training succeed or fail. This is especially true in the beginning stages of training. It is the assistant's job to keep the dog interested and build excitement, thus developing and enhancing the dog's drive to find humans.

The dog must be so interested in the assistant that, more than anything, the dog wants to see where the assistant went and what the assistant is doing. The timing of the assistant's response to the dog is critical to success. However, not every assistant is experienced, so if your assistant is new to SAR dog training, it is important that someone with experience explain to him what to do and how to do it. Sometimes that instructor is you, the dog handler. Without a good assistant, the success of the training session may be compromised.

Equally important is the level and type of praise that the dog receives from both the assistant and the handler. Some SAR

If trained for wilderness work, SAR dogs should be trained to work in and around helicopters so they will be comfortable when it is necessary to be airlifted to search areas. A Colorado Flight for Life helicopter in Aspen, Colorado, provides training for Karla Wheeler and canine Casey Jones.

dog handlers feel that the most important praise is the praise that comes from the assistant because this is what motivates the dog to find people.

No one disagrees that the SAR dog must receive a great deal of praise for the exercises; however, the amount of praise required may vary with each dog. It is important to understand that some handlers are very low-key, and this may result in low-key, unmotivated dogs. Although it may be hard to imagine, some people find it difficult to praise their dogs with emotion. For those people, reward-based training using food may work the best.

While it is rare, there are dogs that are so work-motivated that as soon as they understand what is expected of them, they do not want praise. To them, working is their reward. It takes someone who understands dog behavior to be able to recognize this trait in a dog.

The Observer/Flanker/ Field Technician/Spotter

The observer is critical to the success of all searches, especially so with water, cadaver, and disaster searches. This is because in some situations it takes more than one person to triangulate the location of an alert. The observer also acts as a safety officer, watching for dangers that may not be visible to the dog handler and other rescue personnel, and looks for subtle body language from the dog that the handler can miss. This person must be highly trained and qualified to operate in the field. Although observers are not always dog handlers, their job is equally important.

Training Considerations

All levels of training, except for the very first problems, are conducted in all but extreme weather conditions for the area. This is also true for the tests. The dog must learn and feel comfortable working in all kinds of weather. This will also give you an opportunity to test your clothing and gear. Working in extreme weather on a search mission is not the time to find out that your boots are not waterproof or your parka is not warm enough.

It is essential that a dog and handler be proficient at each level of training before moving on to the next level. At this stage of training, you must make a decision about whether there will be physical contact between the dog and the missing person. Some handlers do not want their dogs to make physical contact with people that they find. The reasoning for this is that on an actual mission, the searchers do not know what mental state the missing person will be in when found. The missing person could be afraid of dogs and become traumatized by the dog. The missing person could hurt the dog, or even kill the dog, such as what happened to Barry, the famous Saint Bernard. This is a real danger if the team searches for missing hunters who are likely armed.

On the other hand, it is essential that the dog clearly show you where the person is located when the person is hidden out of sight. If the dog does not go right up to the missing person, it is possible that the distance between the dog and the person will become so great that you will not be able to pinpoint the person's exact location. Consider the small child asleep or unconscious in dense brush at night. Searchers have walked by people in this situation.

It is quite normal for a people-loving SAR-dog-in-training to rush to the assistant and make physical contact, often lavishing kisses on the assistant. It is also difficult to teach the dog not to make contact when the assistant must reward the dog as part of the training. Handlers must decide which way they want to train their dogs.

My husband and I have elected to teach our dogs to make physical contact. It has been our experience that the dog settles down with time and does not make contact with a missing person the same way that he did in training with the assistant. We have never had a situation where we have felt that our dogs were at risk of being injured by a missing person, and the dogs seemed to sense when to approach and when not to.

If you elect not to encourage the dog to make physical contact with the missing person, the dog should not be afraid to approach strangers. The dog must be confident about people and avoid contact only as a matter of training and not out of fear or caution.

SAFETY TIP

Be sure to assess each problem and allow the dog to have whatever rest and water he needs. However, it is not a good idea to feed or overwater a dog while he is working. Working on a full stomach in some dogs can cause gastric torsion/bloat, a serious safety consideration. Check with a veterinarian for more information about this problem and how likely or unlikely your dog is to suffer from it.

WIND, SCENT, AND DOG

Dogs are experts at finding and identifying scent, but in order for dog and handler to work as a team, the dog handler must understand how the conditions at the time of the problem control the scent. Since humans cannot see scent, we have to rely on our understanding of the weather conditions to determine where the scent is most likely traveling. This chapter will explain how the weather affects scent.

What Scent Is the Dog Looking for?

Before we talk about the nature of scent, it will help the dog handler to understand the two classifications of scent that a dog is trained to find. One is a specific scent, such as what the scent-specific dog is taught to find. This is an individual's unique scent. The rest of scent work involves a *type* of scent. For example, the

An example of how the scent cone from a person rises and spreads.

airscenting dog is taught to find any human scent in an area. It does not matter whose scent it is, as long as it is human. Cadaver and human-remains detection dogs are taught to find the scent of human decomposition. Again, it does not matter to whom the scent belongs, as long as it is human scent. Arson, bomb, termite, agricultural, and other types of detection dogs are taught to find a certain type of scent that may involve a number of different substances that have common elements. On the flip side of this, SAR dogs are taught to ignore classes of scent, such as the scents of animals—all animals (see Game Chasing in Chapter 19).

When the SAR dog handler understands these concepts about scent, it's easier for him to understand how dogs

can be taught to identify a range of scents. It is also humbling to realize the high level of scent discrimination that the dog has the potential to perform.

The Nature of Scent

We cannot smell what a dog smells, but we can help a dog find available scent. To do this, a handler must understand the nature of wind, weather, terrain, and time delay. These elements dictate how much scent is available and where it travels. The handler's ability to put these pieces together will determine how well the dog will perform.

Although many studies have attempted to identify exactly what a dog smells when he follows scent, nobody knows exactly what a dog detects. Dogs can detect

Much like water, scent will flow down a slope, following a path of least resistance.

scent that is diluted one part per trillion; therefore, it is likely that they can identify all of the chemicals/elements that make up any given scent. An odor does not smell the same to a dog as it does to us. For example, if hand lotion were made of pure rose oil and glycerin, we would only smell the rose oil. The dog would smell the oil, the glycerin, and any chemical changes that occurred in the processing of the product, not to mention the smell of the container and who handled it.

Dog handlers can get very passionate about scent theory. Therefore, we will discuss the most popular theories. One theory is that tracking dogs do not follow human scent at all; instead, they follow crushed vegetation and disturbed earth, which is why they cannot follow the trail of a person over hard surfaces.

Others feel that a dog follows dead skin cells, which fall off a person constantly. The longer the person stays in one place, the more concentrated the scent is because the skin cells have collected. Still others feel that a dog detects not only skin cells but also the gasses that the body gives off.

The most important thing is that what a handler believes about scent theory will determine how the dog is trained. The handler's belief about scent theory will determine what he uses as the scent source, where he works the dog, and how

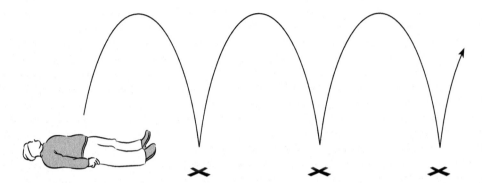

Scent can rise from its source, return to the ground—forming a scent pool—rise again, and fall. This is called looping.

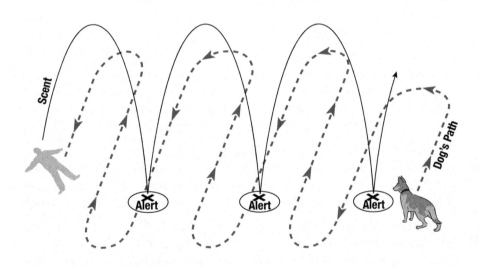

When scent loops, the dog may miss some of the scent pools and find others. By determining the wind direction and pattern of alerts, you can determine from which direction the source of scent is most likely coming.

he works the dog. The safest way to handle the unknown is to assume that all theories are true and give the dog a chance to try all conditions. You will soon learn what your dog can and cannot do.

When SAR people talk about scent, they often speak of the scent cone given off by the human body. The scent cone theory explains that the human body is the source of the scent, or the tip of the cone. As the scent travels away from the source, it fans out to form the base of the cone. As it travels further from the source, the scent becomes weaker or the wind spreads it in an irregular shape. The dog will find this scent and work back and forth, testing the air, until he arrives at the tip of the cone, the source.

In many ways, scent acts the same as a liquid. Scent flows down a slope, following the path of least resistance, such as a gully or drainage ditch. Scent, like liquid, will travel more easily over flat surfaces than heavily vegetated ones.

Scent can also behave like smoke—rising from its source, reaching a high point, and then looping back down to the ground to collect in one area. This cycle can repeat itself, leaving spots of scent spread over an area with "dead," or clear, areas mixed in. This results in a collection of scent pools with no obvious path to the scent source. Handlers who encounter this can become very frustrated, wondering why their dogs cannot find the scent or appear to find and lose it repeatedly.

Sometimes, if the scent source is in a depression, such as a small valley, the scent can travel up the nearby slopes in

When the scent source is in a depression, the scent can rise up the slope. This often occurs during the day, when warm air will carry the scent up.

much the same manner as smoke goes up a chimney. This is often caused by the rise of warm air during the day, which carries the scent with it.

The reverse can happen, too. As the air cools and falls to the low areas, it carries the scent down with it. The scent can be trapped in drainage areas or go from a high area to a low one. When this happens, the scent can pool in a low area. In situations such as these, the handler must understand the weather, wind, and terrain features to try to determine what is happening. In many cases, the IC at base will plot the "hits" or "finds" on a map and see a pattern, helping teams find the missing person.

Terrain features such as tree lines, rock walls, and plowed fields can cause scent to eddy, swirling around trees, behind walls, and over walls, and leaking into cleared areas. On dry, hot days with no noticeable breeze, the scent may rise straight up, and the dog will not find the assistant or missing person unless he stumbles upon them.

In rough terrain and in gusty, shifting winds, the scent can travel in many directions, collecting in nooks and crannies, bushes, and weeds in the same way

Both manmade and natural obstacles can cause the scent to eddy and swirl.

Scent can travel down a slope and collect in a low area. The highest concentration of scent will be in the scent pool in the low area.

that debris is washed down a river. Scent clings to objects such as walls, brush, or low areas. If an assistant or missing person is hidden in dense vegetation, especially vegetation with low, broad leaves, it is possible for the scent to become trapped with little or no leakage. Sometimes the scent will hit a tree, travel up the tree into the air, and not come down again.

Humidity increases the availability of scent for a dog, and scent that has dried out during the day may revive in the damp of evening or morning or after a light rain. The dampness releases and encourages bacterial growth. However, in all probability, a downpour will wash the scent away.

The best time to search with a dog is early morning, evening, or night. The scent is most available at these times. The poorest time for a dog to pick up scent is during the day. Of course, this can depend on the time of the year and the weather for the search area.

In the morning, as the ground warms, scent will rise because scent from warm objects or areas rises in the cool or cold air. In these conditions, it is best to work the dog above low areas so he can detect the rising scent. This time is also excellent for scent-specific (trailing/tracking) dogs because the warmer air from the ground rises but the still-cool morning air holds the scent closer to the ground.

In the evening, the opposite takes place as the higher areas cool and the scent is

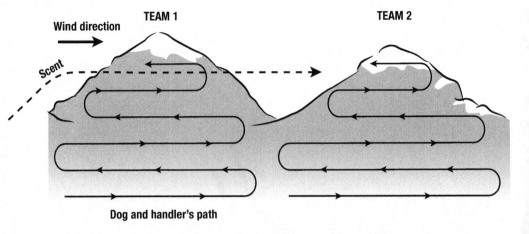

TEAM 1　　　　　　　　　　　　　**TEAM 2**

Wind direction

Scent

Dog and handler's path

Cold air above and warm air below can cause a scent band to form. The dog will hit on the scent in the scent band. By recording the alerts of different teams working along the scent band, the incident commander will be able to determine where to concentrate the search effort.

carried down to the lower areas. Sometimes the scent will travel down, rise a little, and then return to the ground. This is a good time to use the dog because most of the available scent will be at ground level. The best place to use the dog is in the low areas so that they can detect scent that is traveling downward from higher elevations.

If there is a cold layer of air with warm air beneath it (the conditions that cause smoke to hang around in the air and smog alerts), the scent will also rise and linger. A dog working in these conditions on flat ground may have difficulty detecting the scent. A dog working on a hillside or mountain may detect the scent within the scent band and then lose it. It is up to the dog handler to report this to the IC, who will plot the hits on a map and use this information to guide teams to the best area.

What many dog handlers do not realize is that if a person is hidden long enough and the scent collects in one area (saturating the area), it is possible for a dog to have difficulty locating the scent source although he can locate the collected scent. An example of this would be when a person is hidden in an old building, where the air is stagnant. The dog can detect that the person is in the building but may have difficulty locating the specific spot where the person is hidden. This is especially true of less experienced dogs.

When a person is asleep, very still, or unconscious, the body will give off less scent then if the person were moving. If the person has taken shelter in a tent, sleeping bag, or plastic bag, the amount of scent that can escape is even less. If the air is very still and has been since the person was reported missing, there may be a very small scent pool, and the dog may miss it. This is why it is critical that a handler be knowledgeable about scent conditions; he needs to know where to send the dog to effectively cover the team's designated search sector.

Conversely, a moving person has increased sweat (thus more scent), and his sleeves and pant legs can create a billowing effect, puffing scent outward from his body. In addition, a moving person—especially one who is fleeing or frightened—will produce more adrenaline and, thus, more scent.

As the scent travels over an area, the terrain features can create "dead spaces" to which no scent has been carried. These dead spaces are in tucked-away areas that the wind has bypassed. A dead area might be at the base of a sheer cliff where the wind blew off the top of the cliff and angled down, missing the base. Another

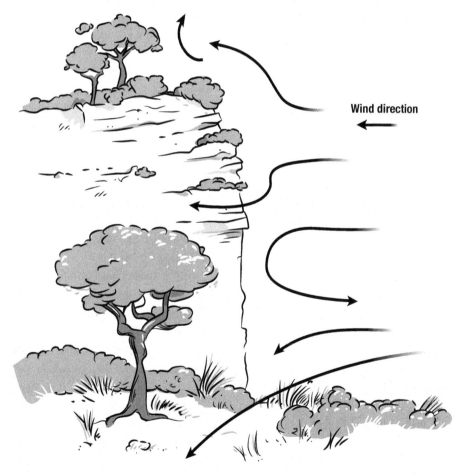

Wind direction

If the wind is blowing into an obstruction (manmade or natural), the scent can be scattered.

type of dead space can occur when the breeze is strong enough to carry the scent over depressions instead of into them. If a dog who is working well seems to lose the scent, let him cast about or quarter back and forth to try to find it; if he cannot, move on a bit, and the dog might find the scent again.

The way scent travels and its availability depend on the weather, terrain, age of the scent trail and source, condition of the scent source, air flow and wind, vegetation, concealment of the scent source, time of day, and time of year during which the dog is looking for the scent. The combination of all of these factors makes each situation unique. It is up to you to determine the conditions so that you understand what the dog is doing in different situations.

You must constantly analyze each situation to understand what the dog is communicating and why. This way, you will know in which direction to keep searching to find the missing person. Never forget that you and your dog are a team; each member of the team has his own job and area of expertise. The dog can never do more than indicate that scent exists in a specific location. It is up to you, and the IC at base, to determine how everything adds up.

Test the Wind

When training for SAR work or on an actual mission, it is essential to know what the wind conditions are. How strong is the wind/breeze, in what direction is it blowing, and how is it acting? Many exercises in this book will need to be set up according to the direction of the wind. There are a few tried-and-true methods to test the wind, and a dog handler needs to know how to use all of them.

- Use a cigarette lighter. By watching the way the flame moves, you can see even the slightest breeze. Be sure to check the wind at the dog's nose level as well as at your eye level, as it can differ at those two locations.
- Hold a piece of thread or flagging tape at both your eye level and the dog's nose level. Some people tie it to their wrist or just under their knee (the dog's nose level), so that it is handy at all times.
- Fill a small compressible object, such as a nasal aspirator for babies, with powder, flour, or cornstarch. By blowing a puff of white into the air, the direction and strength of the wind is visible.
- Set off a small smoke bomb, such as the kind available around the Fourth of July, after the dog has completed a training problem to see exactly where the scent traveled. The smoke bomb should be set off exactly where the assistant was hiding. This way, both you and the assistant can see how the scent traveled and how the dog responded to the scent. Sometimes this method will explain why the dog was not able to find the scent or why the dog worked the way he did.

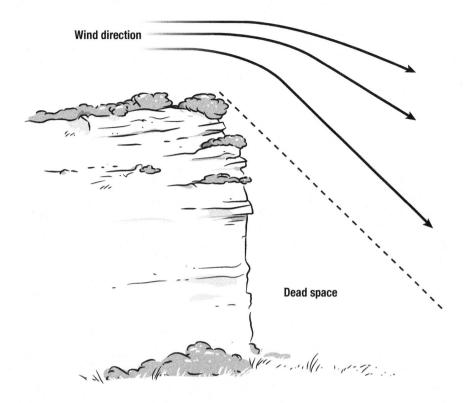

Wind direction

Dead space

When scent is scattered over land features that drop suddenly, there can be a dead space next to the drop.

Each wind-testing method has its pros and cons; sometimes a combination of methods is a wise choice. However, never use a lighter in a disaster situation or where there might be flammable gas or other risks of fire.

As a rule, the SAR dog handler will work the dog *across* the wind, which means with the wind hitting the dog's side, or perpendicular to the direction of the wind as the dog moves into the wind. The dog will quarter back and forth, which will allow him to test the wind from a large area. This method gives the dog the best advantage of finding the scent cone.

Once the dog finds the scent cone, a well-trained dog will work the scent to the source. With a steady breeze, working the dog into and across the wind, a dog/handler team will be able to detect the source of the scent. However, in variable wind conditions and over rough terrain, the source of the scent can be difficult to determine. In variable wind conditions, the handler may have to make the grid pattern much smaller, which can mean that the search area will be reduced or that the team will have to occasionally adjust its search pattern.

PART TWO

TRAINING

THE ALERT/ INDICATION AND ALL- CLEAR SIGNAL

The *alert*, or the signal that the dog gives to the handler, is an essential form of communication between the handler and the dog. It is the only reliable way for the dog to tell the handler that he has found what he is trained to find. It is equally important to be able to tell if there is no scent in the search area. The *all-clear* signal will ease the stress that handlers often have when they clear an area and find nothing. It is a way for the dog to reassure the handler that they didn't miss anything. This chapter will cover both the alert signal and the all-clear signal.

General Concepts

There can be two phases to the alert signal, depending upon how the dog is trained and used. A dog that has been taught to do a refind will give a signal to his handler that he has found the missing person and then give another signal to show the handler where that person is located after leading the handler to the missing person.

Some handlers like to use the same signal for both, while others like to teach two different signals. In many cases, the dogs will settle this matter themselves! Also, some handlers use the term *alert* to refer to both signals while others use the term *indication* for the signal a dog gives upon returning to the handler after a refind. For literary ease, we will use the term *alert* here to apply to either signal. The training method is the same for both.

The alert is nothing more than a signal that the dog gives to his handler to let the handler know that he has found someone. Many SAR dog handlers have strong opinions as to what this signal should be and how it should be executed. There are considerations that each handler must make when deciding which type of alert to use. However, most SAR handlers agree that the signal must be readable in all conditions, as search conditions will vary. For example, the handler must be able to recognize the alert at night, when the dog may be only partly visible or not visible at all. The alert must be detectable when noise, such as that of high winds, is a factor.

The alert is a signal that the dog gives only when a missing person or the target scent is found. Reading the other clues that your dog gives you is another issue. Some dogs will give a lesser signal when they find scent in a scent cone or they find objects. However, the alert for the actual human find must be unmistakable.

The most reliable alert is one that the dog likes to do and is natural for the dog. Remember, the dog will have to use it when exhausted, when frustrated, or in unfavorable conditions. The alert can be a body bang, where the dog hits the handler with part of his body; a tug on a specific object; or a tug on something the handler is wearing. It can be a bark or a retrieve such as a bringsel (an object attached to the dog's collar that he puts in his mouth to signal a find) or a stick. The only limitation is the imagination of the handler and dog. Many dogs will invent their own ways to communicate with their handlers.

One alert that is not acceptable is urination or defecation. Some dogs will do this, but it is not a reliable alert and also can contaminate the area.

It is acceptable and very useful to teach a dog more than one type of alert that the dog can use to indicate different situations. This is one way that dogs can be cross-trained to do a variety of SAR jobs. It is not unusual, out of enthusiasm, for a dog that has one signal for one type of searching to add another signal. Therefore, a dog can have a main signal and a secondary signal that accompanies the main signal. Often this is a special little "dance" or some other form of body language.

You must consider all aspects of the alert and how it can be applied to or hinder various field conditions. For example, some dogs have invented alerts in which they pick up a stick that's near the assistant. This will work as long as there is something to pick up near the assistant. Dogs have delayed going back to their handlers for want of a stick. This can present a problem that must be addressed in training. You also must take care that the dog will not "self reward" (find an object to play with as his reward instead of waiting for his reward) in search situations.

No matter what type of alert is used, you must still learn the dog's body language when working. There is no shortcut for this. You have to watch the dog work and be aware of different situations so that you are able to identify the dog's body language and what it means in each situation.

All of the mechanics of the alert must be taught outside of SAR training. The middle of an exercise is not the time to teach the alert. The purpose of the SAR lesson is to teach the dog when to apply or use the alert. An easy way to teach the dog an alert is to use clicker training methods. Because there are many detailed videos and books about clicker training, these methods will not be covered in this book.

The False Alert

The false alert is every handler's biggest fear, next to missing the assistant or lost person. False alerts happen for a number of reasons. Often a handler's excitement and desire to have his dog perform correctly will cause him to give the dog unintentional signals with his body language. This is easy for a handler to do when the handler knows where the assistant is hiding, because as the dog nears the assistant, the handler anticipates the find. Because dogs watch us very closely, trying to learn and do what we want, the dog could get the wrong message about the training and give an alert based on the handler's body language instead of the actual find. From the dog's point of view, he is doing exactly what he has been taught to do. In some cases, the dog will not find a hidden assistant unless the handler knows where the assistant is hiding.

An example of sending the wrong message is when the handler points to the location of the hidden assistant and leads the dog in and then gives the dog the command to give the alert. Alternatively, the handler may lead the dog to the specific area where the assistant is

ALERT ITEM

If the alert involves the dog's tugging or otherwise handling a special item on the body of the handler, and that item is lost on a mission or for some reason is unavailable, the dog is now faced with a situation where the alert mechanism is not available. The handler must not allow this to happen to the dog.

Giving a good, strong bark alert. Border Collie Lelija is with the German Red Cross Search Unit of Hamburg (Rettungshundestaffel Deutsches Rotes Kreuz, Hamburg-Altona).

hidden, not allowing the dog to search the whole area.

In these cases, the dog learns that the handler does all of the work, and then the dog will not work without the handler's direction. Most of the time, the handler does not realize that he is giving hidden signals. The best ways to avoid this problem are to always let the dog lead and work the exercise out by himself and to have an observer watch how you and the dog work, checking to see that the dog is working on his own.

The observer or unit trainer will routinely test dog/handler teams and watch for this problem by having the handlers work problems in which they do not know where the assistants are hiding. A handler that cannot solve a problem in which he does not know the assistant's location may not trust his dog. Learning to trust the dog is essential for a SAR dog handler.

The assistant or observer can help the dog handler break counterproductive habits by watching for the handler's unintentional signals. Often, if a dog has been responding to hidden signals from his handler, and the handler corrects this, the dog may give a weak or false alert. This happens because the dog is now working under new rules and may be unsure.

Another reason why a dog may give a false alert is that the dog wants the reward so much that he learns to give the alert to get the reward. One way to solve this is to be sure to only give the dog his reward when you are next to the assistant. This way, the dog will work to get you to the assistant/lost person to get the reward.

The best way to avoid false alerts is to teach the dog to give an all-clear signal. This also gives you extra assurance that the dog is doing his job. Teaching the all-clear signal is discussed in the following section.

Types of Alerts

It is important for the SAR dog handler to decide which type of alert he wants to use for SAR work. The dog must then be taught how to execute the alert signal before it is applied to search problems. This way, the dog is not expected to learn two things at the same time.

Method 1: Bark Alert Type 1 (Find and Refind)

The bark alert is a convenient alert because it is easy to teach to a dog and it does not require special equipment. As long as the dog can bark, he can give the alert. Once the dog has been taught to bark on command, you can add this to the find and refind scenarios.

To teach this alert, as soon as the dog finds the assistant and returns to you, immediately give the dog the *speak* command. When the dog barks, give him a small treat or pat on the head and say "Show me." At this point in training, the

dog will know what *find*, *show me*, and *speak* mean. You are only stringing them together to make the dog understand what to do. In most cases, the dog will quickly learn to sequence these commands and perform them on his own. With this type of bark alert, the dog only barks when he returns and before he does the refind.

Method 2: Bark Alert Type 2 (Remain with the Missing Person)

With this type of alert, a dog does not do a refind but stays with the assistant or lost person and barks until his handler arrives. This method works well for disaster work and in areas that are small. In vast wilderness areas, it may be difficult for a handler to hear his dog at a distance. The handler not only has to be able to hear the bark but also must be able to determine from which direction the sound is coming.

To teach this type of alert, first teach the dog to speak on command. Once the dog will speak on command, have the dog bark when he locates the assistant. The assistant may have to tease the dog to get him to bark or give the dog the *speak* command until you arrive. Once the dog barks, you run in to the dog and assistant, at which time the dog gets the reward. Sometimes the best way to get the dog to bark is to make the assistant inaccessible to the dog; the dog can see or scent the assistant but is not able to reach him. (See Levels 2–4 in Chapter 15.)

Method 3: Bark Alert Type 3 (Find and Refind)

This type of alert combines the first two methods. The dog will bark when he finds the assistant and then when he returns to you. Most dogs will do this on their own, but if yours does not, the assistant will give the dog the *speak* command and then ignore the dog when he does bark. Because the dog has been taught to return to you, he should need no, or very little, coaxing to leave the assistant and return to you and bark. As soon as the dog barks, you run with the dog to the assistant, and both of you praise the dog.

Method 4: Physical Alerts

Again, the mechanics of all types of alerts must be taught before being applied to the search scenario. If you want your dog to jump and hit you with his paw, much the same as how a hearing dog alerts his owner to sound, you must first teach the dog the physical act and then incorporate it into the search scenario.

A NOTE ABOUT BARK ALERTS

If the dog is tired from working long distances and for a long time, it may be difficult for the dog to sustain continuous barking until the handler arrives.

Some of the physical alerts are:

Body bang—the dog will hit the handler with a part of his body. Keep in mind that large dogs do not realize that they can hit hard. Handlers have been knocked over by enthusiastic body bangs.

Jump—the dog will jump on the handler in the same way that dogs jump on people when they greet them.

General tug—the dog will pull at the handler's clothing wherever he can reach or grab. It will be done in an obvious manner.

Specific tug—the handler teaches the dog to pull a specific item that the handler always has on his person. This can be a rope tied to the handler's belt or some other object.

Method 5: Retrieve or Bringsel Alert

With this method of alerting, the dog will either find something to pick up and bring to the handler or use a bringsel. Both methods have been popular since World War I for Red Cross/casualty dogs.

The bringsel is an adjustable piece of leather attached by a strap to the dog's collar. This method requires the dog to be comfortable having the bringsel hanging from his collar and carrying the bringsel in his mouth. The dog also must know the *fetch*, *take it*, and *hold it* commands prior to SAR training. (See Chapter 18 for how to teach these commands.)

Prior to SAR training, teach the dog to find and pick up the bringsel. A one-word

The bringsel is an adjustable piece of leather attached to the dog's collar. When the dog finds a person, he will put the object in his mouth and carry it to the handler.

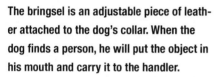

The bringsel type of alert.

command makes it easier to teach the dog how to use the bringsel in a search problem. Start by teaching the dog to pick up the bringsel and carry it to you. This will introduce the concept to the dog that he must carry the bringsel. Next, attach the bringsel to the dog's collar and command the dog to take the bringsel in his mouth and carry it to you. When the dog masters taking the bringsel attached to his collar in his mouth and bringing it to you, it is time to have the dog use it in a search problem.

You will instruct the assistant to hide about 50 feet away. It does not matter whether the dog sees the assistant hiding or not. The assistant will have the bringsel. When the dog finds the assistant, before the dog can leave to get you, the assistant will offer the bringsel to the dog without comment or fanfare. At that moment, you will give the dog the command to bring the bringsel. If the

dog understands that he has to carry the bringsel back to you, it should only take a few sessions for him to understand that when he finds the assistant, he brings the bringsel back to you.

Once the dog knows this, you will attach the bringsel to the dog's collar and set up the same problem. Some dogs can go right to having the bringsel attached; it will depend upon the dog.

If the alert object is not a bringsel, the same training method applies, but without the object attached to the dog's collar. During the two World Wars, dogs successfully learned to take objects from soldiers and bring the objects back to the medics. These objects would be anything that the dogs could find or pick up.

A potential problem here is that the dog may not be able to find anything near the missing person to take back to the handler. Dogs have tried to pick up logs for want of a stick. If the dog tries to take something from a missing person who is awake, the person could mistake it as an attack. Not everyone realizes that the dog is a search dog.

Method 6: Alert Object

This method is very similar to the retrieve/bringsel alert. The main difference is that the dog returns to you and takes an object from you. It is essential that you always have the object available. Attaching a rope or something similar to a belt will work, as long as the rope is accessible to the dog no matter what you are wearing, including a parka, rain gear, and so on.

Again, you must teach the dog how to grab the object on command before incorporating it into search training. Once the dog knows to take the object, he will find the missing person, return to you, and then you will tell the dog to grab the object so that the dog learns to associate a find with grabbing the object as his signal. Once the dog does this, you will give the dog the *show me* command.

When the dog grabs the object, it must be a signal rather than a play session. It is critical for the dog to understand that this signal is not an end-of-exercise signal and that the exercise is not over. This could be a problem for a handler that uses a tug-of-war game as a reward for the dog at the end of a training session.

Using an object in this way can be risky. For example, a handler might use a bandana in his pocket for the dog to grab, but an object attached to or carried by the handler can be lost in dense brush or simply fall out of a pocket. It is critical that you think through this type of alert system.

Method 7: Natural Alert

The natural alert refers to the special body language or action that the dog gives when he has found a person. There is no particular alert per se, although some dogs will naturally sit or lie down. The natural alert requires that you pay close attention to the dog at all times, especially during training, so that you can see the alert.

Most dogs act differently when they have found something. They may hold their ears in a special way, wag their tails, or perform any combination of body language. Some dogs dance with excitement or walk in a unique zigzag pattern. Some dogs have very animated body language while others are very subtle. It can be difficult to tell when a dog is only looking or has really found something, which is why it is so important to study and know the dog's body language.

All handlers must be able to read their dogs. However, using the natural-alert method is extremely risky because many handlers cannot read their dogs well enough to detect the subtle differences in body language. This type of alert will most often cause a handler to miss the assistant or a real missing person.

A natural alert also requires that the dog always work within sight of the handler, limiting the dog's ability to range. This is not practical on most searches. However, this alert does work in situations where the handler stays very close to the dog, such as fine, cadaver, and disaster searching. Handlers who use this type of alert typically do not have their dogs return for refinds, although some dogs will do refinds on their own. It depends upon the dog and the handler.

The All-Clear Signal

Often a dog will give a false alert in order to get the reward. One way to eliminate this is to teach the dog to give an all-clear signal. This way, no matter whether or not the dog has a find, he gets a reward. Some handlers like to use the all-clear signal because it helps ease the stress of not being sure whether or not the dog missed the scent or person who is lost.

Goal

To avoid false alerts by having a special signal.

Target Skill

The dog will give a special signal when he has cleared the area.

Method

The all-clear signal must not be a signal that is used for any other type of search function. The different types of alerts can be modified for this purpose. Take the dog to a small area that has not been used in the last week for SAR training. It should be an area that is not saturated with human scent; therefore, a playground is not an option. Send the dog into the area on a *find* command. When the dog returns to you after he has worked the area, command him to give the all-clear signal and reward him. Repeat this exercise until the dog understands that he is to give the all-clear signal when he has cleared an area.

Problems

The most difficult part of this training is making sure that the dog has a clean area in which to work. If the dog does not seem to understand the exercise, find a different setting. Sometimes using an abandoned building or part of a building that is the size of a small room (approximately 9' by 12') with debris in it will help the dog understand. Be sure that whatever command you use for *find* is one that the dog clearly understands is for people finds, not object finds.

Test

Take the dog to an uncontaminated outdoor area no more than a quarter of an acre in size or an area of approximately that size inside a building. Send the dog on a find search for humans. After the dog has cleared the area and returns, he will give the all-clear signal.

CHAPTER 8

WILDERNESS TRAINING: AIRSCENTING

efore we get into the specifics, I'd like to start off with a few points to keep in mind. First, it is essential that all training be done in steps. Each step is a building block, forming a solid foundation for the next step. Without the foundation that each step provides, problems will result in the advanced areas of training and in the dog's performance.

Next, the geographic location of all exercises must be changed as frequently as possible, or the dog will learn where the hiding places are located and will not use his senses to find the assistant.

In addition, for all airscenting problems (except Levels 1 and 2), whether or not the dog is allowed to see the assistant leave, encourage the dog to airscent rather than to follow the footsteps of the assistant. This is important at the beginning of training so that the dog does not come to his own conclusion that the

Rapelling down a vertical incline with a German Shepherd in a harness. Wilderness searches can require the dog and handler to do whatever it takes to get to hard-to-reach search sites.

problems are scent-specific and the scent is always on the ground.

Also, it is important that the assistant run away in different directions rather than always in front of the dog; otherwise, the dog may think that the lost person is always in front or straight ahead. Remember, a dog only knows what you show him. However, once the dog is trained, a good search dog will use all senses (including hearing and sight) to find the assistant and will put his nose where the scent is, regardless of whether the scent is on the ground, in the air, or in between.

One way to prevent the dog from always looking on the ground in front of him for scent is to have the dog start the problem from different directions. Arrange it so that the assistant is not always traveling a path in front of the dog to the hiding place.

Before you start SAR training, teach your dog what signals to give when he finds the scent. Read the chapter about alerts first, and then teach the dog the mechanics of the signal/alert before he must apply them. This way, the training will not overload the dog with too much new material to learn right away. This does not mean that the dog cannot come up with a new signal. If that happens, it will be natural, and the dog will make it very clear.

Ranging

As you and your dog progress through the levels of training, it is important to encourage the dog to range away from you, searching for scent. The distance that the dog needs to range will depend on the type of problem, density of the brush, weather, and terrain features. The whole purpose of using the dog's scenting ability is to cover more ground faster than people who do not use dogs. One good, qualified dog team is equal to about thirty searchers on foot. The dog is able to get into places that a person cannot, thereby searching an area more thoroughly.

The dog may quarter back and forth in front of the handler in the same manner that a hunting dog quarters or a stock dog drives sheep or cattle. This is usually the

A Beauceron finds a child in a wilderness search.

way that a dog who works on leash will search for scent. Sometimes, if the dog is off leash, he will circle the handler; this is OK, too. For obvious reasons, the dog should not circle the handler while on leash!

In certain situations, the dog may stay close, in front of the handler, and not range at all. However, this severely limits the dog's ability to find scent on his own. The less the dog ranges, the more the handler will have to walk instead of taking advantage of the dog's ability to look for scent.

In all ranging, the goal is to have the dog work across the wind to catch any available scent. Some people do not want their dogs to check back with them too often, as they feel it wastes the dog's energy. Other handlers want their dogs to keep in touch. At no time allow the dog to take off and not check back with you at all.

Sometimes a dog will range too far, especially if the dog is young and full of excitement. It is never a good idea to let a dog work too far away from you because you may lose track of where the dog is working. It is up to you to cover the search area thoroughly. Knowing were the dog worked is essential.

In situations where the dog is taught to stay with the missing person and bark, a dog that ranges too far may be out of your hearing range, or you may not know which direction the dog took when he located the scent cone. In addition, if the dog becomes injured, you will not be able to locate him. If you wish to use a "natural" alert, meaning that you read the dog's body language, the dog must always be in

Lelija, during search training, showing enthusiasm and drive.

your sight so that you can see the dog's alert and any other subtle signals the dog may give.

Correcting a dog that ranges too far is done in a separate training session apart from SAR work. The goal of that lesson is to set boundaries around you for the dog. Once the dog knows the boundaries, they can be applied to SAR work.

Some methods to teach ranging boundaries are:

• While on a walk, wait for the dog to go out of your sight and then hide from the dog. When the dog comes back to check on you, you will not be there. This will show the dog that it is best to monitor you more closely.

• Wait until the dog is out of sight and then backtrack from the spot where the dog last saw you.

• Keep calling the dog back to an acceptable range when he gets too far away. If you always recall the dog at a certain distance, he will learn what his limits are.

Never discourage a dog who is hot on a scent or following through on an alert. Ranging problems are not the focus of training when a hidden assistant is involved. At some time or another, you will miss the dog's alert and could mistake the initial find as the dog's going beyond the range limits when in fact he is making a find.

The other side of the ranging-too-far issue is that the dog that will not leave your side. This dog is not useful to SAR work because he cannot find a scent unless you are right there, which means that you must do all of the work except detect the scent. Sometimes a dog that will not leave your side will not follow through on a scent cone to lead you to the assistant. It is OK to give such a dog a chance to change, but after a few lessons, it might be wise to eliminate the dog from the training program. Dogs that range too far will usually slow down but dogs that will not leave their handlers typically lack the drive and boldness that make a good SAR dog.

One of the reasons why a dog may not want to leave his handler is because he has been trained too strictly in obedience and lacks the drive or confidence to make decisions on his own. This type of dog is always looking to his handler for permission and direction. This can even be a mild form of separation anxiety. If that is

At the start of a mission, ready to search.

the case, the dog will get worse with age unless the handler consults with a good canine-behavior consultant.

A handler who talks to his dog too much can encourage and even inadvertently teach the dog to stay close. Often, handlers are not aware that they are doing this. Therefore, it is a good idea to have an observer watch you and your dog work. If you talk to the dog too much, the dog may become confused and freeze up, thinking that there are more commands that he does not understand.

Once you've given the dog the command to search, do not talk to the dog anymore except to redirect him when necessary. If you are not sure if you talk too much, carry a tape recorder and listen to it after the training exercise. It will quickly become obvious if your talking is annoying and/or distracting to the dog and/or the field technician.

To get a close-working dog to leave you, the assistant must get the dog so excited about following him into the hiding place that the dog forgets about you. Then the assistant should reward the dog, because the dog's natural desire will be to get back to you. In this case, you withhold any reward, even if the dog returns to you with a signal, and the only time you will reward the dog is when you are right next to the assistant. This will encourage the dog to bring you to the assistant to get the reward. Follow the dog to the assistant enthusiastically, but at a distance behind the dog to encourage the dog to leave you and go to the assistant.

Level 1: Beginning Runaway

Goal: To teach the dog the command to find humans and to build drive.
Target Skill: The dog will follow the handler to a hiding place.

Method

Unless you are certain that your dog will not run off or wander, this exercise is done on leash. If you want to work the dog off leash, it must be in an area in which it's safe to do so. Remember, at this stage of training, the dog may not have the drive to stay focused on the exercise, especially if he is a young dog.

You are going to do the "runaway," and the assistant will handle the dog. The reason for this is to build the drive in the dog to find a person. The assumption is that the dog will want to find his handler the most. Once the dog starts to enjoy and look forward to the "find game," it should not matter who the dog has to "find." Keep in mind that at this level we are building the dog's basic concept of searching.

For optimal success, the dog must be firmly bonded to you. If the dog is shy or fearful of strangers, he must get to know and feel comfortable with the assistant before training sessions begin. On the other hand, the dog must not feel so attached to the assistant that he does not want to leave the assistant to find you. These problems are usually associated with very young dogs or dogs that were recently adopted from a shelter.

The main goal of this exercise is to teach the dog that when given the *find* command, he must locate a hidden person. Because this is the dog's introduction to SAR work, it is important to set up the exercise correctly. What the dog is first taught will typically stick with him, even if the methods and rules are changed later. If properly planned, though, the methods and rules will stay the same.

Before you set up the problem, check the wind to be sure it is blowing from the person to the dog, even though this level of training is visual for the dog. You want the dog to work into the wind or be downwind from the person he is to find, which means that the wind will be blowing into the dog's face, even if it is just a slight breeze.

The area where the problem is set up must be open, with some brush, weeds, or other places for a person to duck behind and hide. If possible, the ground

Kevin Huggett with four-year-old female Labrador Retriever Bazuka are with the Kittitas County SAR group in Washington.

should be level and easy for the dog (and you) to run over.

The assistant will hold the dog while you stand in front of the dog. While you run away from the dog, acting excited by waving your arms, calling to the dog, and even jumping a bit, the assistant encourages the dog to watch you. The assistant does not give the *find* command during

this encouragement. After you cover 50 to 100 feet, duck behind an object while the dog is watching. (Note that you must be easily accessible to the dog once he reaches the object that you are hiding behind.)

At the moment that you disappear, the assistant will give the dog the *find* command and either release the dog or run behind the dog if the dog is on leash.

Be certain that the assistant gives the find command before the dog is allowed to take off after you. The dog should be given the *find* command and released at the peak of his excitement. If the assistant waits too long, the dog may lose interest. It's also important to note that if the dog is on leash, the assistant must be careful not to tug on the leash in a manner that the dog will interpret as a correction.

Remember, it is important that the assistant release the dog at the height of the dog's excitement and drive to find you. Make sure that the distance and exercise will be short so that the dog does not lose interest or curiosity. At this point in training, the dog is not being taught search skills, so he does not have to think about or guess where you are located. Because this is a visual exercise, the dog must be able to run right to you.

When the dog reaches you, both you and the assistant reward the dog using what the dog likes best. This can be food, a toy, a game, or a click and treat. (If using clicker-training methods, the click will have been established before this exercise. You must know how to use clicker training before starting SAR training.)

If the reward is food in conjunction with a reward game, be sure to focus on the game rather than the food. This way, the food can be eliminated when the game is sufficient as a reward.

This exercise is continued until the dog gets excited and barks to find you as soon as he knows that the game is about to begin. You will recognize this by how hard he pulls and tries to get away from the assistant to find you. When the dog is consistent, and both you and the assistant are certain that the dog anticipates the search game each time you do this exercise, then it is time for the next level.

It usually takes five to seven sessions, one a day, for a dog to learn this Level 1 exercise. This exercise is the foundation for the *find* command, so do not rush the dog. Some dogs can handle two or three runaways per session, but to avoid the possibility of a negative reaction to training, two or three per session are the maximum. It is OK to train the dog every day if the training location can be varied enough.

Some handlers feel that they do not want their dogs to learn a visual find because the dogs will be weaned off it later. In this case, the problem would be set up so that the dog cannot see exactly where you finally hide. The dog always sees where you ducked out of sight, he but will have to look for a very short distance to find you. You must be within three or four seconds of travel time for the dog; the hiding place must be easy for the dog to find, not deep in an obstacle. Remember, the dog is not learning search skills at this level, only that the command given means that he is to find a human. The goal of this

Note: Some handlers/trainers like to have the dog's handler act as the missing person well into the training. They feel that this builds a very strong search drive in the dog.

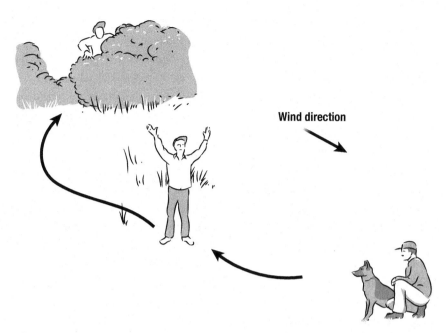

Wind direction

The assistant runs from the dog and hides in a way that will keep the dog's attention.

exercise is to build drive and make SAR work fun. It is essential to always end the exercise with the dog's having a happy, fun find and getting plenty of praise.

Problems

A problem sometimes encountered by a dog/handler team and assistant is that if the dog is very young, he may not run right in to the handler, especially a partially hidden handler. There are a number of reasons why this happens:

1. The dog may be too young for the training and/or cannot focus long enough. In this case, the dog is distracted by other things, including the scent of other animals that may have been in the area.

2. The dog is not bonded to the handler enough to care where the handler went. If this is the reason, training should be delayed until the dog is sufficiently bonded.

3. Some dogs are too fearful to go into strange places; such dogs need time to grow and be socialized.

4. If the dog is older, it may be a case in which the dog lacks the drive to look for the handler. If the handler cannot find a way to get the dog interested, then this dog is not a good candidate for SAR work.

If the problem is not with the SAR exercise but due to other issues, suspend the SAR training until the other issues are resolved. Continuing to try SAR training could ruin any chances that the dog may have to be a SAR dog. Examples of some of the other issues that could derail the SAR exercise are lack of control over the dog, the dog's lack of drive as indicated by being distracted from the exercise, and distracting circumstances such as other dogs, people, wildlife.

Many dogs fail at this level. Never forget that dogs have likes and dislikes, and some have no interest in this type of work. To try to force a dog is not ethical to the dog, the unit, or the missing person.

Test: Level 1

The setting is an open area with light brush or an object to hide behind no more than 100 feet away. With the dog on leash, the assistant holds the dog while you run away, not making a spectacle of yourself, but allowing the dog to see you. At this point, it is expected that the dog will show anticipation and excitement while you run away. As soon as you duck behind an object, the assistant gives the *find* command and lets the dog run to you. The dog should go right to you, at which time both you and the assistant reward the dog. The dog must be excited and enthusiastic and must go in to you without hesitation.

Level 2: Novice Runaway

Goal: To reinforce the command to find a human.
Target Skill: The dog will find the assistant instead of the handler.

Method

The conditions for this exercise are the same as in Level 1. If possible, use the same assistant who helped you in Level 1. This can be important for young dogs, who may feel more secure with someone they know rather than with a stranger.

It is important to make a decision about the training at this point. Some trainers feel that it is best for the dog to continue to look for the handler rather than switch to the assistant at Level 2. They feel that using the handler as the hidden person builds a stronger drive in the dog. If you or your unit trainer feel that the dog does not have enough drive at this level of training, it may be a good idea for you to continue to be the hidden person until the dog shows acceptable drive. However, for ease of explanation here, we'll assume that the assistant is the hidden person.

Set up the problem the same way as in Level 1, so that the wind will be blowing from the hidden person to the dog. The assistant will do everything possible to tease the dog and keep his attention as the assistant runs away to a hiding place at a distance of 50 to 100 feet. (Some trainers feel that if the assistant isn't making a fool of himself in enticing the dog, the exercise is not being done right. In addition, be sure that the dog's praise is lavish.) The area should be relatively flat and easy for the dog to run over. As soon as the assistant ducks behind an object, you will give the dog the *find* command and release him. Again, as in Level 1, be very diligent that the dog is given the command to find at the instant *before* being allowed to run to the hidden person.

Problems

You may find the dog to be reluctant to go to the assistant. Using the same techniques as outlined in Level 1, the assistant (the person hiding) will encourage the dog to make contact by luring the dog with either a toy or food. It is very important at this stage of training for the dog to understand that contact or getting very close to the person hiding is essential. Even if you do not feel that the dog has to touch the assistant, future problems can be avoided by letting the dog learn now that contact is part of the requirement.

You must never lead the dog in to the assistant. If the dog thinks that you will lead, this will cause problems later that are very difficult to fix. You can encourage the dog to make contact with the assistant, but do not lead the dog in. Specifically, "leading the dog in" means that the handler is physically in front of the dog and makes contact with the assistant

first. You must also avoid pointing to the assistant because the dog will learn to wait until you show him where to go.

As soon as the dog gets close enough to the assistant to see the reward (a toy or food), the assistant can reach out to the dog to lure and/or tease the dog with it. Once the dog sees that there is nothing to fear, this should not be a problem again. If the dog is very young and shows fear at this level of training, go back to Level 1 (with you hiding) for a few weeks. When the dog is working confidently at Level 1, try Level 2 again.

If the dog does not get over being unsure of going in to an assistant (keep in mind that the person is not fully hidden at this point in training), give serious consideration to eliminating the dog from the program.

As the excitement builds, the timing of the reward and play is essential. The assistant can sit facing the dog with a tug toy held motionless against the assistant's chest for the dog's play reward. As soon as you are next to the assistant

SCHUTZHUND AND SAR

It is my opinion that no dog that is Schutzhund-trained (trained as a protection dog) should in any manner be used as a SAR dog. It is asking a great deal of a dog to determine what is and what is not a threat when the behavior of the missing person could be hostile, erratic, or highly excited. If the dog has been trained for personal protection work or bite work of any kind, it is essential at Level 2 to teach the dog that a "hit" (biting the assistant) is not permitted. Some SAR dog handlers feel that a dog should be Schutzhund-trained to do SAR work, and this is the point in training where the distinction must be made clear to the dog.

with the dog trying to get to the reward, the assistant will reward the dog. Again, at this level, we want to introduce to the dog that you need to be next to the assistant for the exercise to be finished. This concept is important, and reinforcing it strongly at the beginning of training will help avoid problems later.

Test: Level 2

Stage the test in an open area with light brush or objects for the assistant to hide behind. The assistant will run into the wind (the wind blowing toward the dog). With the dog on leash, you will encourage the dog as the assistant runs away. The assistant will not try to attract the dog as he did in training but will quietly and quickly run about 50–100 feet away and then hide. As soon as the assistant is out of sight, you will give the *find* command and let the dog run to the assistant. Stay a little bit behind the dog to allow him to lead and go in to the assistant first.

The dog should stay focused on the assistant, demonstrating a high level of excitement as soon as the assistant leaves and until the dog is released on the *find* command. Finding the assistant should make the dog happy.

Level 3: Intermediate Runaway

Goal : To solidify the dog's desire to find a human.
Target Skill: The dog will find an assistant when there is a slight time delay.

Method

For this problem, ideally the assistant is someone the dog does not know. The problem is set up in the same way as in Level 2, and the dog is worked on leash unless the dog has been trained to work off leash by this time.

The assistant will walk away without acknowledging the dog in any way. You will stand quietly and let the dog watch the assistant walk away. This is one way to see how excited the dog is about the search game. The dog should react with a high level of excitement.

Wait one or two minutes after the assistant is hidden before giving the *find* command and letting the dog go. Let the dog work even if he acts calm while the assistant leaves. Do not try to get the dog excited. Some dogs will contain themselves until they are told to find. If the dog does not get excited on the first try, you can psych him up just a bit on the second try after the assistant hides. Because this problem is executed a bit differently, the dog may be slightly hesitant. However, if the dog is jumping and barking, do not correct the dog at all. Quietly hold the dog until it is time to find.

As the dog progresses with the short delay, increase the time that he waits to find the assistant up to five minutes, but no more. When timing the delay, use a watch; do not depend on your sense of time, as it is rarely correct, and time is important in this exercise. At this level, you must be sure that the path to the assistant is not always in front of the dog.

In addition, at this level, the assistant can move a short distance from where the dog saw him disappear.

As the dog works, depending upon the weather and wind, he will start to quarter (range back and forth for about a quarter of a circle) in front of you. If the dog is not certain about how to do this, you can walk the pattern to show him, making sure that he ranges in front. When the dog finds the scent cone, searching will become natural. Ideally, the dog will quarter and search for the scent on his own.

Problems

A young or immature dog may not have a long enough attention span to keep his mind on the task for the five-minute delay. Dogs that are four months old or older can usually handle the delay if they have worked up through the levels. If your dog is not able to handle the delay, do not push him; go back to a shorter time delay that the dog can manage and gradually add more time.

The assistant can also make a noise or call the dog if needed to get the dog interested. This should be a short noise or call, not a continuous one. When the dog makes a find, both you and the assistant can reward the dog. If the dog tends to do his *find* exercise and then go exploring, he must be worked on a long leash. Never allow the dog to wander.

Test: Level 3

Set up the test in an open area with a light breeze blowing from the assistant to the dog. The area will provide adequate cover for an assistant to hide easily. The brush may be a bit denser than in Levels 1 and 2.

You will wait quietly while the assistant walks away to hide. It is OK for the dog to be excited, and it is also OK for the dog to behave in a calm manner as long as he stays interested in the problem.

After a five-minute time delay, give the *find* command and follow the dog in to the assistant. The dog should run right in to the assistant without hesitation. The dog must not wander around the area, but should be focused on finding the assistant. When the dog makes the find, he is rewarded.

Level 4: Advanced Runaway

Goal: To reinforce the *find* command for finding a stranger and to heighten the dog's anticipation and drive to search.
Target Skill: The dog will work off leash and find the assistant without watching the assistant run away.

Method

Start this exercise with the dog on leash. The assistant (ideally someone the dog does not know) will hide about 100 feet from the starting point. The wind will be blowing from the assistant's hiding place to the dog. Do not psych the dog up or let the dog watch the assistant go to the hiding place.

As soon as the assistant is in position, he will radio you to tell you that he is ready. If you can watch the assistant and be certain when he is in position, no radio contact is needed. The assistant should be as quiet as possible. You will wait up to five minutes before starting the problem. After the time delay, send the dog out on a *find* command to look for the assistant.

As the dog successfully finds the assistant, start to increase distance (size of the search area) and time. However, you should increase only distance in one problem or series of problems, and then only time in another, or vice versa. Never increase both distance and time in the same problem. As the dog becomes more focused on the exercises, start working off leash if you haven't already done so.

At this point in training, you must always know where the assistant is hiding and when the dog finds the assistant. The use of two-way radios will make this easier. The assistant must never call to you (voice or whistle) to let you know that he is in position and ready for the dog to make the find, because the dog will use this sound to locate the assistant and not develop his search skills.

This point in training is critical to prevent bad habits from forming. Some dogs will start to do refinds on their own by this stage of training. If your dog does this, count your blessings and encourage him. If the dog's signal is to stay with the assistant and bark, the dog should start doing this.

When the dog works well off leash, encourage him to range and work the grid pattern with you. Once the dog finds the scent cone, he will learn on his own how to work the wind.

At this point in training, you may have to encourage the dog to search in thick brush, because it is natural for the dog to want to go around it. Now is also the time to start using directional signals with the dog. However, this is not the time to teach these signals, as the dog should have already learned them in a separate exercise. Using directional signals at this point is meant to give the dog practical experience in applying them.

Problems

A possible problem is that the dog could miss the assistant because the exercise has been set up so that the dog has to rely on his sense of smell rather than both smell and sight. Many conditions affect scent: time of day, weather, time of year, humidity, contaminating odors, distracting odors, etc. Depending upon the weather conditions, the scent could be looping, blowing in an erratic manner, going straight up, and so on. The dog could also miss the assistant because the scent cone is not available for him to find due to the aforementioned factors. This is why it is very important for you to understand how scent behaves.

If the dog misses the assistant in a reasonable amount of time, let the assistant make a noise so that the dog can have a

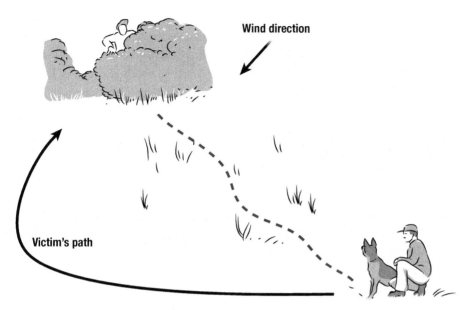

Wind direction

Victim's path

In the intermediate runaway exercise, the assistant quietly walks away and hides, taking care not to walk in a straight line from the dog to the hiding place.

find. Then set up the problem again, being mindful of the wind.

The dog may also miss the assistant because the dog is not motivated enough to find a person. If this is the case, go back to Level 3 and try again. If the dog continues to lose drive when he cannot see the assistant run away, the dog may not be a good SAR candidate.

Another problem could be that the dog gets distracted by animal scents. If this happens, and you are certain that it is animal scent distracting the dog, redirect the dog by giving him the *find* command and encouraging him to go in the direction that the assistant went.

Do not assume that human and animal scents have not mixed. It is important to be certain that you are not correcting a

dog who is following human scent. Keep in mind that it may be impossible for you to be certain that no other human has been in the training area during the hours before training or that an animal did not run through the area. If the dog insists on following animals, refer to the section on game chasing in Chapter 19. If the dog will not give up following animals, then the dog is not a good SAR candidate.

The dog may find the assistant and then take off, assuming that the problem is finished. If this happens, put the dog back on leash and start over. Reinforce for the dog that the reward does not come until you and the assistant are together. When reworking the dog to solve this problem, you must try to get to the assistant as quickly as possible for the dog to get his

Once the dog has a find, the dog should immediately return to the handler to give an indication. The excitement in this dog is obvious.

reward. As the dog responds and makes the connection that you and the assistant have to be together, delay your arrival a tiny bit at a time so that the dog makes the connection that he may have to wait for you to arrive to get the reward.

Test: Level 4

Set up the test in a relatively open area with light brush, with the breeze blowing from the assistant to the dog. The assistant will hide about 100–200 feet from the starting point. The dog does not see the assistant leave or hide, and the dog may enter the test area from another direction than the assistant did.

When the assistant is hidden and about five minutes have passed, you can start the dog on the search. Grid the area while the dog starts to range to pick up the scent and look for the assistant.

When the dog finds the assistant, he should go in without hesitation to the as-

sistant. If the dog does not exhibit drive, misses the assistant, follows non-human scents, or hesitates to go directly in to the assistant, go back to Level 2 or Level 3 until either the problems are resolved or a determination is made that the dog is not SAR material.

For the entire test, it must be obvious that the dog is working to find the assistant and using his nose.

Level 5: Beginning the Refind

Goal: To train the dog to return to the handler after finding the assistant.
Target Skill: The dog will lead the handler to the assistant to get his reward instead of being rewarded right away.

Method

The exercise is set up the same way as in Level 4. The dog is sent out to find the assistant, but this time you will walk very slowly so that the dog is ahead of you, about halfway between you and the assistant. This will encourage the dog to work away from you and make him feel as though he is leading.

When the dog finds the assistant, the assistant will ignore him instead of giving him the reward or acknowledging him. It is essential that you know exactly when the dog has found the assistant so that you can watch what the dog does. If the dog does not come back to you on his own as soon as he realizes that the assistant is not going to acknowledge his presence and reward him, you will call the dog to come back. The moment that the dog returns to you, he must give you an alert/indication signal, which you've taught him prior to this point in training. Initially, you may have to ask for the alert until the dog automatically gives it after a find. As soon as the dog gives the alert/indication signal, you will give the dog a refind command, such as *show me*. By using a new command instead of the *find* command, the dog will understand that you recognize that he has found the assistant.

As soon as the dog starts to lead you to the assistant, you will run excitedly behind the dog to show him that he's doing a wonderful job. To behave otherwise, such as moving slowly behind the dog, will discourage the dog and lessen his enthusiasm, perhaps even undoing the training up to that point. Once you are next to the assistant, the dog gets lavish praise from both of you, solidifying to the dog that he has done a great job.

Problems

One problem is that the dog may not return to you when called but will stay with the assistant. To correct this, you will get very close to the assistant before calling the dog to come to you. If the dog makes even a slight move toward you, praise him and run to the assistant. As the dog gets the idea, increase the distance between you and the assistant.

Another way to solve this problem, for a dog that is strongly bonded with you,

is to duck out of sight (the same as in the puppy games) and, when the dog runs to you, you and the dog both return to the assistant. This method works best in situations where the dog may think that you are close enough to the assistant for the problem to be finished. A dog who is rewarded too soon by the assistant and before you are right next to the assistant may think that you do not have to be next to the assistant for the exercise to be over.

A different method would be to put the dog on a long leash and work through the problem. If you decide to use a long leash, care must be taken so that it does not get tangled. It will give the dog the wrong message if you have to jerk on the

This dog is encouraged to find the victim and then return to the handler.

Note: By now, the dog will have worked through the runaways and be ready to move on to giving the signal. In the initial runaways, the dog may not have done a refind on his own. Many dogs will refind without being specifically taught. If yours is not doing refinds, this is when you prep him for the find and refind. Before the dog is asked to give an alert signal, he should know to return to you and lead you back to the assistant. Once the dog can do that, add the signal. Some people teach the alert first and then do the refind training. If you plan to teach your dog to stay with the missing person and give a bark alert instead of doing a refind, you can skip the refind traning.

To avoid future problems and ensure a correct response, the dog must go directly in to the assistant on a find, immediately return to you, and then lead you directly to the assistant. He must not stop, wander, play, or otherwise be distracted. Do not start this phase of training until the dog is obedient enough to work off leash and be under your control. If the dog has already started to do a refind on his own, you will refine the steps at this point.

It is important in many of the exercises that follow that you know when the dog has found the assistant. One way the assistant can signal to you without talking is to key the microphone on the handheld radio. This way, you will know that the dog either is on his way back to you or was distracted after finding the assistant.

It's also important to note that if the dog is not excited or interested in SAR work by this level, it's time to dismiss the dog from the program.

leash to untangle it, because this could be mistaken by the dog as a correction. Do not use a long leash more than a few times to show the dog what is expected of him. Voice control, motivation, and bonding are the key elements for success with this exercise.

Do not give the dog a correction if he does not come back to you. Instead, obedience practice is in order. The dog may wish to stay with the assistant because this is the person who has been rewarding him. If the dog realizes that you have the reward, he will catch on quickly.

Another problem is that the dog may find the assistant and then either take off in pursuit of animal scents or just wander around as if the exercise is finished and he is free to play. This can happen because the assistant is not interesting enough to the dog, but usually because the dog thinks that the exercise is over as soon as the assistant has been found. The methods just discussed typically will solve this problem. However, if the dog is more interested in finding animals and consistently follows animal scents, proof the dog against this. (See

Chapter 19.) Sometimes the solution is simply to reinforce the desired behavior and build motivation in the dog. Food or a more enthusiastic play reward may work. Again, using the long leash may help by giving you more control over the dog.

Test: Level 5

Set up the test in light brush or woods, with the breeze blowing from the assistant to the starting point. The assistant is well hidden, and the area is large enough for the dog to have room and time to work out the problem.

After the assistant is in place, let the assistant sit and cool the area for at least fifteen to thirty minutes to let the scent spread from the assistant's path and to let the scent cone build up. Then you will send the dog to search. The dog will work at least 50 feet from you, ranging or quartering as you work a grid pattern.

The dog will alert as taught and not deviate from it, even if you can find the assistant without the dog. This is a test of the dog's training more than a test of the dog's search skills.

Level 6: Advanced Refind

There are two schools of thought about this phase of SAR work. One teaches the dog that the find and refind are one operation and that the entire exercise is not over until the handler is right next to the assistant. This method uses a *show me*

command, which tells the dog that the handler recognizes the alert/indication and that the dog must bring the handler to the assistant. The second concept is that the dog does a find over and over until the handler is next to the assistant. In essence, the dog does the find repeatedly until the handler gets to the assistant or missing person.

In light of new research about the intelligence of dogs, the second method might be frustrating to the dog, as he is finding the same person repeatedly. The dog will know that he has already found the assistant and could become confused when asked to find again, thinking that there is a new person to find. Thus, the second method could lead to misunderstandings for the dog when more than one person is lost. From the dog's point of view, it is most likely less confusing for the find and refind to be one complete action.

Goal: To teach the dog that the handler does not always "see" the assistant and that the dog must be sure that the handler locates the assistant.
Target Skill: The concept described in the goal will be solidified for the dog.

Method

Once the dog consistently returns to you after a find and gives a reliable signal, the *show me* part of the exercise is strengthened. A dog has no way of know-

Searchers are dropped off by helicopter to search for a missing hiker. King County SAR, Washington.

ing that you cannot smell, see, or hear what he does. Therefore, it is up to you to teach the dog that humans generally are blind and deaf, with a lousy sense of smell. This will ensure that in a situation where you are standing next to the missing person, the dog will keep insisting that you go in to the missing person (think small toddler curled up asleep in dense brush). The dog must understand that even though you may be just a few feet away from the missing person, you do not know that the missing person is nearby. The dog must not think that you are aware of the missing person and are walking away, as this would teach the dog that it is OK to walk away from a missing person, thus contradicting the

main reason for using dogs in SAR.

Initially, the exercise is set up in an area of about 50–100 feet so that the steps of the exercise will occur quickly in succession. The size of the area is adjusted based on how fast the dog works an area.

The assistant hides without the dog seeing him leave, and then you send the dog on the search. When the dog finds the assistant, the assistant ignores the dog. You will allow the dog to complete the alert and refind, but when you get to the assistant, you will hang back just a few feet. You will not look at the spot where the assistant is hiding and will act as though you are still searching. You will give the dog the *show me* command again so that the dog stands almost pointing from the assistant to you with his head. Sometimes you must frustrate the dog a bit to get the dog to insist that you move right next to the assistant.

As soon as the dog shows you, while you are close to the assistant, both of you will lavishly praise the dog. As the dog gets the idea, make the dog "show you" a few times before acknowledging the assistant.

Once the dog does a good job of insisting that you be next to the assistant, carefully introduce the idea to the dog that you do not think the assistant is there. Do this by starting to walk away, and as soon as the dog tries to bring you back to the assistant, turn and run to the assistant; both of you will praise the dog. Increase the distance until the dog will not let you leave the area without going to the assistant. This type of training will go a long way to prevent handler error in the field.

Problems

The dog may think that the exercise is over when he either finds the assistant or returns to you. If this happens, withhold praise until the dog leads you to the assistant. Sometimes teaching the dog the *go to* exercise can help clarify the *show me* concept. If the dog returns to you and does not lead you right back to the assistant, commanding the dog to go to the assistant may help. If the dog cannot master this, go back to the previous level of training and work up to this level again.

Test: Level 6

Set up the problem so that the distance is far enough where the dog must work for at least twenty minutes in order to find the missing person. When the dog finds the missing person, you will walk in such a manner as to indicate that you do not know that the dog found the missing person. The dog will return to you, give an alert signal and then lead you to the missing person.

Scout returns to Susan Bulanda to lead her to the assistant.

CHAPTER 9

ADVANCED WILDERNESS TRAINING

The purpose of the advanced levels of training is to practice search techniques, perfect dog/handler skills, and test the dog/handler team's ability to search. This stage enhances what the dog has learned up to now. The dog previously learned the mechanics of searching, and now he will learn search skills and how to apply the mechanics to real scenarios. Dogs, like people, need time to practice their skills so that they can learn how to use them in various situations. This is why a seasoned dog/handler team is poetry to watch. This is also the phase of training where the bond between dog and handler develops into a genuine team effort.

Remember, you are not teaching mechanics in this phase of training. If the dog has a problem ranging, searching, performing maneuvering skills, or doing the find, alert, indication, or refind, go back to the previous levels to solve these training issues before progressing. To do otherwise could cause the dog to fail.

In the advanced levels of training, the assistant can hide in any number of places, not just brush and woods. For example, farms often have areas in which old broken equipment and vehicles are disposed of, as well as crumbling barns and storage sheds. Even on wilderness searches, a team can encounter debris piles and junk piles. On a mission, a dog/handler team will have to search these areas.

Success in helping a dog become a master searcher comes by giving him the opportunity to solve problems on his own at this level of training. This means that you do not micromanage your dog. A handler who micromanages—that is, tells the dog what to do at every step of the problem—does not trust his dog. This will hinder the dog's ability to learn how to use the wind and weather to its best advantage. Never forget that no handler has the ability to smell and hear what the dog smells and hears. Trying to tell a dog how to do his job is ludicrous.

General Rules for Area Training

After a handler is assigned a search area and has identified his boundaries, he will review the area on a topographical map. The handler must know the terrain features in order to plan a search strategy and determine how to travel in the area. The handler will take into account the weather and wind direction and try to position the starting point in a way that will give the dog an advantage. Terrain features will help the handler determine the width of the grid pattern. The density of the brush, the woods, the weather conditions, and the obstacles encountered, as well as how far the dog will range and the direction of the wind, will all play a part in how the handler will work the problem. If the brush is so dense that scent could be trapped, the dog/handler team may have to walk tighter or smaller grids. If the area is open with a nice breeze, a larger or wider grid may work.

In rocky and hilly terrain with many features that can channel scent, the dog may need to work closer to the handler so that the handler can be certain that the dog investigates all of the terrain features. A young, excited dog may overshoot areas where scent can pool, while a slower, more experienced dog will know to check these areas and will search methodically.

In dry, hot, still conditions—especially in high grass, weeds, or dense vegetation—the dog may need to work close to the handler. The scent can rise straight up in these conditions, and it is easy for the dog to miss the scent unless he walks right over it. This means that the grid pattern may have to be very tight.

Each search is unique and requires that the handler analyze the conditions for each area. Sometimes the way the dog works or does not work will be a reason to reassess the situation. However, keep in mind that the focus of training exercises is to allow the dog to learn how to work in different search scenarios.

The major mistake that almost all new

handlers make is that they want to micro-manage their dogs. As I've mentioned, this stifles the dog's ability to search and use his mind. The less a handler directs and talks to his dog, the better. In order for a dog to learn, he must be allowed to make mistakes, explore, and try different things. Dogs can think, so if your dog's training up to this point has been solid, and he knows what to do and what he is looking for, he will learn how to do it on his own. A good handler will not try to tell a dog where to put his nose or how to do his job. Never forget the *team* part of teamwork.

Level 1: Trail or Hasty Search Training

Goal: To develop the dog's search skills and to begin conditioning the dog for area problems.
Target Skill: The dog will find an assistant in a short wilderness/trail setting.

Method

Again, the dog will have learned all of the mechanics of searching by this level. If he has not, go back to the level at which the dog needs help and work up through the levels again.

The search area will be a wooded/brushy area approximately one-half mile long, with a dirt road or trail through it. The assistant will hide no more than 20 feet off the trail. The assistant will not always walk along the trail to get to the hiding place; this will show the dog that not every physical trail is a scent trail. It is not unusual for a missing person to avoid a trail or not be aware that a trail is nearby. Therefore, the assistant will vary the path of travel, walking the trail some of the time and walking off-trail other times.

It is important for you to know where the assistant is hiding so that you can study the dog's behavior and recognize if the dog has strayed from or misses the scent. You will pay close attention to the dog to learn the dog's working style and body language, such as his excitement when he picks up the scent. His excitement may show in the form of a little "dance," a certain way he carries his tail, or another type of physical clue. This is also a good time to look for and correct any blossoming bad habits before they become unmanageable.

Once the assistant is in place, you will send the dog to search. The dog should range 50 feet or more, show enthusiasm, demonstrate that he is working, and be under control. The dog will find the assistant, give an alert, and perform a refind if that is how the dog is trained. It is a good idea for the unit trainer to periodically test your team to make sure that you are not leading the dog or cueing the dog in any way, to build your confidence in the dog's ability to search and find, and to evaluate your ability to read the dog.

Problems

Provided that all of the previous levels of training have been mastered, there should

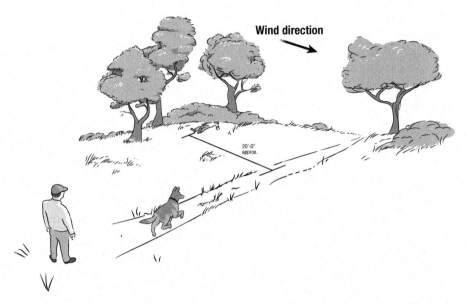

Wind direction

20'-0"
approx.

Trail exercise: the assistant is hidden approximately 20 feet off to the side of a half-mile-long trail.

be no major problems with the mechanics of searching at this level. However, different problems, such as game chasing, may occur. Another problem that can surface is that the dog may begin to run off because of his enthusiasm or his new-found freedom. As always, go back to a previous level to work through any problems.

This is the point in training at which you may be so desirous for your dog's success that you may begin to unintentionally lead the dog, giving him clues as to where the assistant is hidden. It is the job of the unit trainer or an experienced observer to watch for this.

Test: Level 1

The test is set up the same way as the Level 1 training session. The assistant will hide

at least 60 yards upwind from the starting point. Once the assistant is ready (quietly notifying the observer by radio), you will wait to start the problem to let a scent cone develop. The amount of time will depend upon the weather conditions. Once the conditions are right, you can start the exercise. You will decide how to enter the test area. For the test, you will not know where the assistant is hidden; this way, you will learn to trust your dog.

The dog will show a strong desire to work and not hesitate when sent out on the *find* command. He will range freely, his distance determined by the type of terrain. The dog should be able to respond to your directional commands so that you can keep him in the test area. All of the mechanics of searching should be almost flawless.

As the dog learns how to manage this type of exercise, practice in situations where there is no hidden assistant. You and your dog must be confident that you cleared the area and did not miss the assistant. This is essential for you to learn to trust the dog's ability both to find the missing person and to determine when there is no one to be found in a given area.

Level 2: Beginning Area Training

Goal: To teach the dog/handler team to search a larger area and for the team to gain search experience.
Target Skills: The dog will be able to search larger areas and will display heightened anticipation and endurance for wilderness searching.

Method

Do not attempt this level unless your team has successfully mastered the previous levels and reliably demonstrates the mechanics of searching (ranging, alert, refind, etc.). This is the level at which you and your dog will perfect your searching skills. The dog will learn how to work the wind to its best advantage, and you will continue to learn to read the dog.

This problem will start with an acre of land and work up to 10 acres. Once in a while, you will not know where the assistant is hidden. However, the observer will always know the location of the assistant.

This will help you gain trust in your dog and become aware of any weaknesses in the training methods.

For the first problem, the assistant will maintain a distance of at least 100 yards from the starting point. The dog must demonstrate the drive and skills to handle the problem. As the problem is repeated (over different training sessions), the distance, density of the brush, and difficulty of the terrain are increased to replicate an actual mission for that area. The dog must willingly work through thick brush, in woods, over hilly and flat terrain, in water, and in open fields with distractions.

This is the point in training where you introduce the concept that a person could be up or at an elevated level. This is easy to do by having the assistant hide in a tree or another place that is higher than the level at which the dog is searching. If the dog seems to have difficulty understanding this concept, the assistant can make a quick, quiet noise when the dog is looking on the ground underneath the hiding spot. Usually, the dog only needs this help once and then he learns to look up as well as on his own level.

Some dogs seem to enjoy this change in the training scenario and show a heightened level of excitement when the assistant is in a tree or other inaccessible place. This will also strengthen the dog's desire to point or show you where the assistant is hiding.

At this level of training, the assistant can be hidden at ground level but in a spot

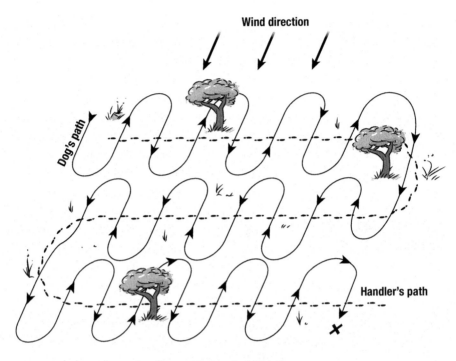

Wind direction

Dog's path

Handler's path

Canine team grid pattern—a zigzag grid to work the wind.

that's not accessible to the dog. This is accomplished by having the assistant buried under debris or covered with brush.

You and your dog must be able to work for at least one hour, but take care not to push the dog, especially if he is under a year old or out of shape. Dogs need to be conditioned just like people do.

It is a good idea to have the assistant make noise once in a while to simulate a person who is crying, injured (moaning), or calling for help. The dog will encounter this on a real mission.

Problems

At the beginning of Level 2, you may believe that the dog is working inconsis-

tently because you may not understand the conditions that the dog is working through, such as wind, scent availability, and weather. This is where an observer will help determine what is happening. If there is doubt as to why the dog seems to miss scent or be having difficulty, check the training log to see how the dog worked in similar weather conditions. (Do not hesitate to set off a small smoke bomb at the completion of the exercise to see what the scent is doing.)

Pushing a dog too fast is another mistake that handlers make. Be sure to let the dog work at the pace that is comfortable for him. Do not try to tell the dog how to do his job. Remember, as the size of the area increases, so must the dog's concentration, determination, and stamina. This requires motivation and conditioning on the part of both of you.

As the size of the area increases, you must pay close attention to how well the dog works and watch to see that the dog is still working and not just walking around. Sometimes it may be difficult to establish when and if the dog stops working. As some dogs reach their pace, they may look as though they are not working when they really are. If there is no scent available, the dog will look like he is walking or trotting, when in reality he is sniffing the air. Only trial and error will help you identify what the dog is doing.

Test: Level 2

Administer this test repeatedly, increasing the size of the test area and in all weather conditions to simulate actual missions. The area size will range from 5 to 10 acres. Be sure that the assistant hides in a location unknown to you.

The dog and you must perform the search without difficulty. The assistant and observer will not break radio silence to assist in any way; however, the observer will know the general, if not specific, location of the assistant. The observer will evaluate the following:

1. Your field safety measures
2. The dog's search skills
3. Mechanics of the dog's alert, find, and refind
4. Your control over the dog

WORK WITH CARE

When working on and over obstacles with a dog who is tired, you must keep in mind that the dog's ability to judge distance and depth are not as good as a human's ability. Be careful!

5. The teamwork between you and the dog
6. Your search strategy
7. The time it took you to complete the mission

Level 3: Advanced Area Training

Goals: To increase the dog's search stamina and level of performance and to solidify the handler's ability to read the dog.
Target Skill: The dog will achieve wilderness-search readiness.

Method

Once the dog can work 10 acres (approximately) without difficulty, it is time to expand the search area. Exercises at this level are treated as if they were actual missions, from the beginning at base to the conclusion, also at base.

At this training level, the person who sets up the problem for your team will be sure to include various clues for you to find. You will know how many clues there are for most of the exercises. However, be sure that if you know that there are five clues, you and the dog do not become lax after finding five clues. Clues are typically pieces of clothing, tissues, gum wrappers, footprints, or anything else a lost person might leave behind or drop.

In most of the previous training sessions, you've known where the assistant has been hidden, but now it is time for exercises in which this information is not available, so you will not know where or if there is an assistant hidden. This will eliminate any hidden signals that you may give the dog.

At this level of training, it is also important for each session to have new situations/conditions/elements to make the exercises more and more difficult. The observer must carefully watch to make sure that you are not so focused on the dog that you miss other clues or fail to consider the physical conditions of the problem such as wind, weather, and terrain.

Additional exercises will be set up in which there are up to three, but no more than three, assistants hidden in one area. Special consideration is given to the placement of the assistants based on the wind, weather, and terrain. You will not know how many (up to three) assistants are hidden or if there is no assistant hidden. This problem can cover up to 1 square mile (640 acres), depending upon the terrain and the density of the brush/woods.

WORKING IN SECTORS

If a number of dogs are working on this exercise at this level, it is a good idea if each team is assigned a sector in the same manner as in a real mission, with only one assistant hidden.

If the problem is one in which there is no assistant to find, the dog will be given a quick problem at the end of the exercise in which the dog has a live find. Keep in mind that this is still training for the dog, so be very careful not to micromanage the dog; let the dog work the exercise with minimal guidance. This is a decisive test of trusting the dog and building the dog's confidence in you.

During these exercises, you will also practice clue-awareness skills, radio communications with base, and topographical map-reading skills, and have a full backpack as required by the unit's Standard Operation Procedures (SOPs), all of which have been taught throughout the training.

Problems

This level is a test of dog/handler teamwork. Dogs will fail at this level for a number of reasons. One main reason for failure is that you tried to take shortcuts when progressing through the training levels. If you tried to train the dog on your own, with only one assistant and always knowing where the assistant was hidden,

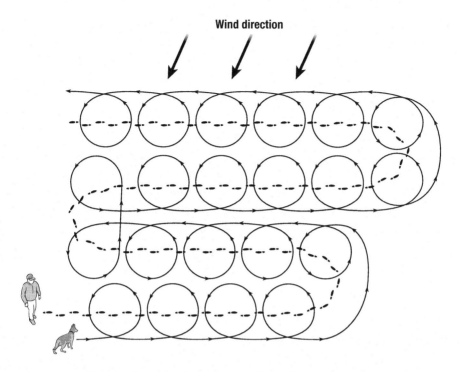

Wind direction

Learning to grid an area based on wind, weather and terrain is one of the key factors in canine SAR. Some dogs will zigzag across your direction of travel while others form a circular pattern; this is called ranging. The object is that your dog searches the area around you for scent.

the dog could have been reading you and not finding the assistant on his own. New handlers often give in to this temptation, consciously and unconsciously, because they are afraid that their dogs will fail.

Sometimes a handler will lose confidence in a dog's ability to do search work. This can happen when the handler (erroneously) decides that the assistant is in a certain place or could not be in a particular location, so he ignores or corrects the dog for giving what the handler feels is a false alert. This will confuse the dog and undo the dog's training. This is especially devastating to a dog that has

been taught to be very obedient.

If it turns out that you are insecure, or that your dog cannot work at this level, go back at least two levels and work up to this level again, focusing on the problem areas.

Tests: Level 3
In all three tests, the location of the assistant(s) is unknown to the handler. The handler will not know how many (zero to three) assistants are hidden.

Test 1: Conduct this test in any weather conditions. The area is from 1/4 square mile (160 acres) to 1 square mile (640 acres) in size. The tester/observer will place one assistant so that you do not know where the assistant is hiding. You will define the search area clearly on a topographical map, identify the starting point based on the weather and terrain features, and outline the strategy for this problem, which will last from six to eight hours in moderate terrain.

Test 2: The same as Test 1, but with two or three assistants hidden far enough apart that the dog will not be able to find them at the same time.

Test 3: The same as Test 1, but with no assistant hidden.

Level 4: Beginning Night Training

Goal: To develop night-searching skills for both the handler and the dog. **Target Skill:** The dog will become aware that the handler cannot see well at night.

Method

Start with an area of about 5 acres in which it's safe to walk at night; this means an area that is relatively flat with no holes, cliffs, ledges, mine shafts, and so on. The area will include light brush, trees, and paths. The assistant will be approximately in the middle of the area, close to a path.

The dog will have a light (it can be a light stick) attached to his SAR vest or collar, and you will be equipped with a headlamp and flashlight according to the

unit's SOPs. For safety reasons, the assistant must have a radio to be able to contact base at all times.

If you wish to teach the dog to work close at night, you will call him back often to show him that working at night means working closer. It is amazing how many dogs will learn to work close at night on their own, but some need to be shown.

Nighttime can be the best time to look for a person who is missing because the weather conditions can be more favorable. (Unfortunately, though, research has shown that from a quarter to up to half of missing people continue to travel at night.) However, this does not mean that the team should wait until nighttime to start searching. Sometimes an IC who is not a rescue person will call the search off for the night, but unless there is danger to the searchers due to terrain features, that is not a wise decision. As mentioned, from a canine perspective, the weather conditions are often the best at night. Searching at night is one example of why you must have a good, readable alert from your dog.

Problems

The dog may not lead you in close enough to the assistant to see where the assistant is hiding. Some dogs can get a little spooked when they do their first nighttime training session. If this happens, and your dog does not recover after one search problem, discontinue working with the dog at night for the time being.

Spend as much time as possible walking the dog at night to calm any fears he may have. If possible, duck out of sight while walking the dog at night, similar to the hide-and-seek games used to teach him to stay close. Once he likes being out at night, the training can resume.

If the dog is slightly unsure of himself on his first nighttime training session, you will withhold the reward until the dog leads you close enough to touch the assistant. Even if you do not want the dog to make physical contact with missing people, he must still lead you close enough to identify where the assistant is hiding. If need be, the assistant can call

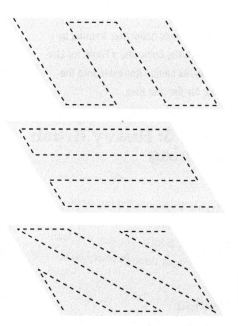

The starting point used to grid a sector will depend upon the wind, terrain and weather. Always start in a location that gives your dog the best advantage.

the dog one time on the initial find. Most dogs catch on quickly.

In some areas of the country, certain types of predators hunt at night. If a dog is usually OK with night training but suddenly behaves in a frightened manner, consider that he may have gotten the scent of a nocturnal predator. In areas where this is possible, you and/or the field technician or flanker may want to have a means of defense against predators.

Test: Level 4

This test will be conducted in fair weather, after dark, in an area of between 5 and 10 acres that is safe to walk in at night. You will decide what equipment to use as well as how to execute the problem. The observer will pay close attention to the way your team works, including whether or not the dog seems to be afraid to leave you, ranges too far, or hesitates to go in to the assistant at any time during the find and refind. It is the observer's job to watch carefully to see how well you and your dog cover your area.

Level 5: Advanced Night Training

Goal: To expand the dog's night-search area and to build confidence between the dog and handler.
Target Skill: The dog's ability to search at night will be refined.

Method

Conduct this level in the dead of night, when there is no glow left from the setting sun. Set it up the same way as the previous level, but with the area expanded up to approximately 40 acres. You will not know how many assistants (up to three) there are or where they are hidden. If your team can handle 40 acres at night, you'll be able to handle the larger areas that may be encountered on an actual mission.

Problems

By this time, most dogs understand that their handlers cannot see at night (imagine what dogs must think of us—not only can we not hear or smell but we're also blind!). Be aware, though, that some dogs still may not understand the sensory limits of humans.

It is critical for night work that you know where the dog is working if he takes off to follow a scent. This requires that the dog work closer at night than during the day. If the dog ranges too far and fast, you can go back to the "hide behind a tree" game with the dog to show him that he needs to slow down and pay attention to where you are.

Test: Level 5

The test for this level is the same as in Level 4 except that the test area is expanded to approximately 40 acres or a little larger.

During dry-land helicopter training in Crested Butte, Colorado, a Flight for Life nurse loads canine Kootenai onto the copter for the first time.

Level 6: Heavy Brush Training

Goal: To expose the dog to heavy brush situations.
Target Skill: The dog will learn how to work through heavy brush.

Method

Set up a problem for the dog in heavy brush. By this time, the dog will be used to working through light brush. Gradually introduce areas where the brush is heavy and allow the dog to find his way into and through such areas. If possible, hide an assistant in heavy brush so that the dog learns that people can be hidden in this type of environment. Always be aware of dangers, such as thorns.

Problems

In certain areas of the country, there are types of bushes, such as mountain laurel, that have very low, broad leaves. These types of bushes will trap scent but, more importantly, they offer shelter to lost people. Large bushes will form tent-like areas underneath them, and children are fond of hiding in such areas. Therefore, the dog must know how to search these types of bushes, but some dogs are afraid to go into them because either they have not encountered them before or they cannot see that there is space inside the bushes.

If the dog is hesitant to go into dense brush, place an assistant whom the dog knows in the brush. Be sure to grid right by the area so that the dog can detect the scent. If necessary, have the assistant call to the dog the first time or two. A bold and confident dog will catch on quickly and learn to search into and through this type of cover.

If the dog encounters heavy brush that is impossible for him to crawl into, he will learn by experience to circle around the brush to look for scent and to alert as close as he can get. If the dog cannot get in, then the assistant can cut away enough brush to crawl in so that the dog will learn to look for scent in these situations.

Test: Level 6

The test is staged in any weather conditions in an area with heavy brush. Use an area between 10–40 acres in size. The dog must search the area thoroughly, and if he cannot go into or through the brush, it must be obvious that he is looking around it for scent.

Level 7: Multiple Assistant Training

Goal: To teach the dog that on any given mission, he may have to find and indicate on more than one person and to allow the handler to see how the dog works this type of problem.
Target Skill: The dog's concept and understanding that there can be more than one person in an area will be reinforced.

Method

Searches can involve groups of people who get lost together. This is often the case when groups of children go camping or hiking. It is important to practice this skill in training.

The observer will place two to four assistants in an area of approximately 1/4 square mile (160 acres). The assistants will be far enough apart so that the dog cannot find all of them in the same sweep; however, if three or four assistants are used, two of them can be close enough to be found together (but not in the same spot).

Once the dog finds the first assistant, you will praise the dog as previously described; then, after a minute of rest, you will command the dog to search again, and the two of you continue. The first assistant found will either walk along with the observer or return to base. If you wish to replicate a real mission, another team can deploy to the location of the first assistant to simulate removing an injured person. In this case, you and the dog will stay in the area until the evacuation team arrives so that the dog can experience this scenario (it will be the first time he is seeing such a scenario with this type of exercise).

Problems

Sometimes the dog will think (based on previous training experiences) that once he finds an assistant, the problem is over. If this happens, psych the dog up the same way as in a Level 1 training session, pointing away from the found assistant. If the dog returns to the first assistant and finds him again, praise the dog (after all, the dog may think that you—being deaf, blind, and scent-challenged—do not understand that the person was already found), but not as enthusiastically as you would for a first find, and then direct the dog to continue.

Test: Level 7

The observer will place two to four assistants in an area of about 160 acres with any type of terrain and any weather conditions. The assistants will be placed in any spatial relationship to each other.

You will outline the search strategy and complete the problem in about five hours, depending upon the terrain. When the dog finds an assistant, you will radio back to base and give the location of the find and the condition of the assistant. Once you finish the entire problem, you will return to base to debrief. At that time, you will be told whether or not your team found all of the assistants, how good your coverage of the area was (you are required to give the probability of detection [POD]), and if you missed any areas.

Level 8: Beginning Moving Assistant Training

It is common on a real mission for the missing person to be mobile in the search area. Occasionally, the missing person will wander unnoticed into the base camp and mingle with the searchers, undetected. More often, the missing person will be confused, in a state of shock, or just trying to find a way back to safety. This is why it is important that the dog has experience in finding a moving assistant. Keep in mind that up until now, all of the training has been with assistants who remain hidden and stationary. The dog could easily assume that all missing people are concealed and quiet.

At times, the dog will find and alert on other searchers on a mission; if that happens, treat it as a normal find. As the dog gains more experience, he will learn to tell who is a searcher and who is not.

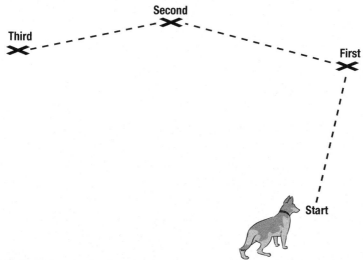

Multiple-victim exercise: in some situations, there may be more than one person lost. Your dog should be able to find more than one person in an area.

Goal: To teach the dog that the assistant may not be where the dog left him.

Target Skill: The dog will find an assistant who has moved.

Method

The training area will have a mix of brush, woods, open areas, and trails. The assistant will avoid the trails and walk through the brush and woods. The assistant can walk through the open areas as needed, but should not hide in the open areas.

As soon as the dog makes the find and is out of the assistant's sight and on his way to you, the assistant will move a few hundred feet and hide in a new location that is upwind from the last location. You will treat the problem as if nothing is new or different. When the

dog returns to the spot where the assistant had been hiding, you will wait and see how the dog handles the situation.

Ideally, the dog will follow the scent to the new location. If the dog is unsure about what to do, you will give the *find* command without pointing in the direction that the assistant went. Let the dog put his nose wherever he wants to. When the dog finds the assistant again, both of you will praise the dog lavishly.

Problems

The dog may give up when he returns and finds the assistant gone. If this happens, recommend or tell the dog to find, getting very excited. Some dogs will do well on a *show me* command.

If recommending the dog fails to motivate him, then you can grid in the direction where the assistant is hidden. The dog will find the assistant and know it was the same person. All the dog has to do is make the connection that sometimes the assistant will move, and he needs to look further.

If this does not work, set up a new problem for the dog and have the assistant move only 10 or 20 feet from the original location. As the dog succeeds, the assistant can move farther away.

Test: Level 8

The test is staged in an area large enough to allow the assistant to move into a new location when out of the dog's sight while the dog is leading you to the assistant. It can be done in any weather, terrain, or other conditions. If the test is done in the snow, be sure that the dog cannot follow footprints. One way to do this is to have the assistant scuff his footprints.

The dog must do the find, alert, and refind as normally done. When the dog brings you to the first place where the assistant was hidden, the dog must then find the assistant again, giving the alert and leading you to the new hiding place.

Level 9: Advanced Moving Assistant

Goal: To have the dog learn that the assistant can be moving.

Target Skill: The dog will find an assistant who is walking, and the handler will gain confidence in the dog under these circumstances.

Method

The assistant will hide in a large area and leave a scent pool by standing or sitting for at least fifteen minutes. The assistant will then start to walk slowly, taking care to mark the area where the scent pool is located and the direction in which he walked away from the scent pool. Leaving an article in the scent pool and making an arrow with rocks or sticks to show the direction of travel is one way to do this. The markings must not be obvious, as you don't want a smart, observant dog to detect it as a visible sign.

You will start the problem as usual, following standard search procedures. The dog will find the scent pool and give a signal. At this point, if the dog is cross-trained to be scent discriminatory, you can use the article left behind and command the dog to find that person. If the dog is an airscenting-only dog, continue to grid until the dog finds the assistant.

The assistant will continue to walk very slowly until the dog insists that you approach the assistant. At that point, both of you will praise the dog.

Problems

The dog may not understand that the walking assistant is the person he is to find. In some cases, the dog may not give the alert signal on a walking assistant. If this happens, you can give a toy or food treat to the assistant and have him reward the dog as soon as the dog makes the find. If necessary, the assistant can squat down and greet the dog, then get up and start to walk away. The dog must understand that the missing person can move, and because the dog has learned in earlier training sessions that the person he is to find can have the reward, this will show the dog that he has found the missing person.

Another way to show the dog this concept is to have the assistant stay in one place until you are in sight. When the dog can see the assistant, the assistant gets up and starts to walk slowly. The dog will know that this is the missing person and that the person is now moving. The dog will bring you to the assistant because the dog will have the assistant in his sight for the entire refind. As the dog gets the idea, work up to the method previously outlined.

Level 10: More Advanced Moving Assistant

Goal: To solidify the moving-assistant find for the dog.
Target Skill: The dog will find a moving assistant in areas where he is not used to finding an assistant.

Method

For the most part, the assistant has not been hidden in open areas or walking on trails. The dog knows this; therefore, he needs to understand that a missing person can be out in the open and moving. On an actual mission, the missing person may find a trail and try to follow it to safety.

This problem is set up the same way as in Level 9, but the assistant hides and then walks into an open area or onto a trail. Once the dog masters one assistant moving in this situation, add groups of people so that the dog will understand that more than one person can be missing and that missing people can be in a group.

Problems

If the dog has difficulty understanding that a group of people can be lost, have four to six assistants sit together, hidden by the terrain features (brush, woods, etc.), and let the dog find them together as a group. After the dog masters this, have the group get up and start walking slowly while the dog does the refind. Use the same method as described in Level 9.

Test: Level 10

The test is set up the same as for Level 8 except that the assistant(s) walk in areas where the dog is not used to finding people.

Note: For all moving-assistant problems and tests, be certain that the distance between you and the assistant is great enough to allow the assistant time to move to another spot before the dog returns on the refind. Mix up the training problems so that the dog will not know if the assistant will move or not.

Advanced Wilderness Training

CHAPTER 10

THE SCENT-DISCRIMINATION DOG

T he scent-discrimination dog is a dog that follows one specific scent identified by the handler. Generally, there are three types of scent-discrimination dogs that fall into this category:

1. Tracking dog—a dog that is taught to keep his nose in the footprints of the missing person.
2. Trailing dog—a dog who works the scent within a specific range (typically a few feet) from the footprints.
3. Airscenting scent-specific dog—a dog who works in the same manner as the airscenting dog (off leash) but will follow the identified scent.

Because there are many books written about how to train the scent dog, we will not go into all of the details; however, we will cover the basic principles of scent work as it applies to the SAR dog.

While you will decide which type of scent-specific

work you want the dog to perform, it is important to consider some facts about dogs and scent. First, you must realize that the dog is a master at detecting scent. If humans could find scent, we would not need to use dogs. *A dog does not have to be taught how to use his nose, only what to look for.*

Next, a dog either has a good nose or he doesn't. No one breed is better than another; it is a matter of the individual dog. The exceptions, of course, are dogs with short noses—brachycephalic breeds such as the Pug, the Boston Terrier, and so on. These dogs have a much-decreased ability to detect scent. However, just because a dog is from a known scenting breed, such as the Bloodhound, does not mean that the individual dog will be good at scent detection. For example, one individual Border Collie may be able to detect scent better than a particular Bloodhound.

Until Level 9 in this chapter, all training will be done in areas that are relatively uncontaminated with human scent. Nevertheless, unless someone has monitored the area, there is no way to be certain what scent conditions exist. Use various types of conditions for training, such as wilderness, woods, or open areas and/or fields. Keep in mind that the best time to train is when there is a little bit of moisture present on the ground, which typically happens in the early morning and evening.

A wise handler will be aware of the different theories about scent and a dog's ability to detect it. Some people claim that a dog does not follow the scent of the person at all, but that the dog follows the crushed vegetation where the person walked. People who believe this theory feel that a dog can identify a particular person by how crushed the vegetation is,

TAKING A BREAK

When training/working with a scent-discrimination dog, if a dog that usually works well is having an "off" day, stop training and check if the dog is healthy and feeling well. If he is healthy, wait for more favorable conditions to resume training or work. If the dog seems to be not feeling well, a visit to the veterinarian may be in order. In any case, the dog should not work again until he feels better. If you are not sure, give the dog the benefit of the doubt and give him a few days off. A dog can feel poorly and not show it in obvious ways.

If you find that a dog who usually works well seems to have lost the ability or drive to work, go back a few levels until the dog can work up to the more difficult levels and succeed. It is always possible that the dog may not understand what is expected.

based on the weight of the person. If a handler believes this, his tendency will be to train his dog to follow footprints.

Other people feel that a dog detects the dead skin cells, known as *rafts*, that fall from the body as the person passes through an area. These people tend to allow their dogs to look where the scent is located. Others still feel that a dog uses a combination of both crushed vegetation and rafts.

Some handlers feel that a dog cannot detect scent on hard surfaces, such as city streets, parking lots, etc. Others believe that a dog cannot detect scent near highways because the fumes from vehicles destroy the dog's ability to detect scent. Some handlers feel that if dogs are confined in areas where there are a lot of fumes, such as in the back of an enclosed truck or the cargo hold of an airplane, that they temporarily lose their ability to detect scent.

However, before you form a solid opinion about scent, consider that a dog can successfully identify people out of a lineup from scent that was collected from a crime-scene object and has been stored for up to three years. The object can be a gun, knife, or anything else used at a crime scene. The only substance that gives off scent that is available to save would be the skin cells and oils from the criminal's hands.

We know today that dogs can follow the path of a person over hard surfaces. This means that crushed vegetation is not available to them to follow, but what is

SCENT AND WEATHER

There are several circumstances that affect a dog's ability to detect scent. First and most obvious are the weather conditions. To read about the dynamics of scent, see Chapter 6.

left are skin cells that have fallen from the person's body.

We also know that drug dogs can detect drugs located in liquid-proof containers and hidden in the gas tanks of vehicles. This means that gas fumes do not prevent a dog from detecting scent.

It bears repeating here that dogs can detect scent that has been diluted to one part per trillion, the equivalent of about one gram, or one drop from an eyedropper, spread over a city the size of Philadelphia. Thus the only real limits that a dog will face are the ones that the weather and the handler impose on him. The wise dog handler will not try to tell the dog how and where to look for scent, only what to look for. If the weather conditions allow the scent to collect 100 feet from the assistant's path, then let the dog seek this out and follow it. Many dogs have lost the trail because they were not allowed to look where the scent was available. They were not allowed to range to locate the scent because of their handlers' preconceived notions about where to look for scent.

So in essence, allow the dog to put his nose where he wants to put his nose. That can be on the ground, up in the air, or anywhere in between. Again, if humans knew where the scent was, we would not need dogs!

This becomes a challenge for some handlers who forget that the most important goal is to find the missing person. In some cases, the missing person may have wandered aimlessly through an area for miles. In the right conditions, the scent-specific dog may detect the airborne scent of the missing person and be able to quickly lead the handler to the missing person without following a mile or more of footprints. The time saved in this situation can mean the difference between life and death for the missing person. It is an example of having enough faith in the dog to allow him to put his nose where the scent is rather than to tell the dog how to follow the scent.

All of the scent-specific exercises in this book assume that the dog is going to be worked in a tracking harness and on a tracking lead. When possible, all training should take place in calm weather conditions. When the training problem indicates that it can be done in any weather conditions, this refers to moisture in the air. A calm, drizzly day is OK, as is a calm, clear day or a snowy, but not too windy, day. Do not put a dog in a weather situation that will cause him to fail. Only experienced dogs can handle weather extremes, both from a scent-detection perspective and mentally.

When starting scent work with the dog, especially if the scent path itself is not long, it may be necessary to have the wind blow from the dog to the assistant (also known as a "butt," or "tail," wind) so that the dog will be forced to look for the scent path instead of airscenting. A tail wind will keep the scent ahead of the dog. This is also known as having the assistant "upwind" from the dog. On real missions, this is not important, because it does not matter how the dog gets the handler to the missing person, but for training purposes it will help clarify for the dog that he is to follow a particular scent. Remember, we are teaching the dog to look for a scent path, not practicing with an experienced dog. Again, and most importantly, we are not teaching the dog how to use his nose, we are teaching the dog what to look for.

The Scent Article

The scent article is a critical part of scent-discrimination training because this is what is used to identify the scent that the dog is to find and follow. Be sure to use different scent articles so that the dog will learn to work from various sources. Initially, you'll use a scent article made of cloth (the kind is not important) so that the article will hold a lot of scent. Later, the dog will be offered articles made of all types of materials, such as metal, wood, plastic, and anything else that you can dream up.

For all basic training, the scent article is as "clean," or as uncontaminated, as possible. This means that the article will mainly carry the primary human scent. It is virtually impossible to have a truly uncontaminated scent article, so we work with the best that we can.

In scent-specific work, it is very risky to give the dog more than one *find* command when on a scent path. This is especially true for dogs that are learning. The "green" dog, the one just starting out, may detect older human scent on the path, and if he is recommanded at that point, he could become confused as to which scent to follow. Therefore, do everything you can to avoid recommanding a dog after he has been started on a scent path.

If you feel the need to encourage your dog while he is working, use a command to tell him to "hurry up" or "stop playing around," but do not use whatever word you've chosen for the *find* command. Telling the dog to "get to work" may help.

It is important for you to approach the start of the scent path from all directions; otherwise, the dog may come to the conclusion that the scent path is always in front of him. In reality, the scent path could be off to either side at any angle. Remember, just as in the other exercises, the dog only knows what you show him. Taking care of details now will prevent problems later.

In real search situations, even though you give the dog a scent article, the scent trail may not actually be in the area that you or the IC think it is in because the point last seen (PLS) or last

known position (LKP) of the missing person may be wrong. Therefore, it is a good idea to teach the dog how to give an all-clear signal. (See the section on alerts in Chapter 7.)

Level 1: Scent-Specific Runaway

Goal: To teach the dog the command to find a specific human.

Target Skill: By first finding the handler and then finding an assistant, the dog will demonstrate knowledge that the object is to find humans.

Method

The technique for training at this level is the same as for wilderness searching. Therefore, you will go back to Chapter 8 and follow Level 1: Beginning Runaway, Level 2: Novice Runaway, and Level 3: Intermediate Runaway. When you and your dog are proficient at these levels, move on to Level 2: Using A Scent Article, which follows this section. While the dog is working on Level 2: Using A Scent Article, you are at the same time teaching a *look* or *take scent* command.

EQUIPMENT

If the dog is going to work on a leash, the leash should be long. The length will depend on how dense the brush or trees are in the area where the dog will work. Generally, a length of 8–12 feet works best. Use a non-restricting tracking harness that the dog wears only when doing scent-specific work. Some handlers put their unit patches or other small emblems on their dogs' harnesses to identify them as SAR dogs.

Use the leash and harness every time the dog does scent-specific work. This equipment serves as a signal to the dog about the type of work that he is going to do.

This command tells the dog to identify the scent from an object or to put his nose to an object.

Food works very well in teaching a dog to look at a specific place. To do this, drop a piece of food on the ground and point to it, giving the dog the *look* command (or whatever word you want to use, as long as it is consistent and not used for anything else).

If your dog has already been taught to airscent, you'll teach him a new alert that he'll use for scent-specific situations. However, a find is a find no matter how the dog does it, so the airscent alert can work, too. If the dog is going to be a scent-specific dog only, you will start to teach the dog the alert signal, which is necessary for future exercises.

Remember, the alert signal is taught as a separate lesson from the scent problem. The dog must know the alert signal before SAR training. The scent lesson is not the time to teach the alert signal, but the time to apply it.

Level 2: Using a Scent Article

Goal: To teach the dog to connect the scent article with the assistant.

Target Skill: The dog will smell the scent article and then use it to find the assistant.

Method

At this point in training, the dog must clearly understand that the *find* command means to find a human. If the dog indicates that this is not clear to him, keep working at the previous level. To push ahead too soon will undo the training you've done so far. Dogs that have already been taught to airscent typically make the transition easily.

The exercise is set up in an area that has light brush or objects to hide behind. The assistant holds the scent article toward the dog and then drops it on the ground. You stand quietly as the dog watches this and then sniffs the article. If the dog does

In the scent-article runaway exercise, the victim drops a scent article for the dog to see, then runs away and hides.

not automatically sniff the article, you can give the *take scent* command. By this time, the dog usually knows that this is a search exercise.

The assistant walks away and hides about 50 feet from the starting point. You will watch the assistant carefully to see exactly where the assistant walked. This way, you can judge how and where the dog detects scent. If it is possible to do so, mark the assistant's path in such a way that the dog will not notice the marks.

It may be necessary for the assistant to hide in a less accessible location to give the dog a reason to look for the scent instead of doing a visual search. The assistant is not within sight of the dog.

Take the dog to the scent article, give the *look* command, and then give the *find* command. If the dog is already airscent-trained, the *find* command for scent-specific work is a different word than the one used for airscenting. The dog will follow the general path that the assistant

made and lead you in to the assistant. When you are next to the assistant, both you and the assistant reward the dog.

Some dogs become so focused on folowing scent that they do not pay attention to their handlers, so handlers usually work with their dogs on long tracking leads to keep up with the dogs. A handler should never pull a dog off a scent path, as this is counterproductive to training.

In the beginning levels of scent training, it is essential that you are careful not to let other odors contaminate the scent article. This includes the scent of the container in which the scent article is stored. To prevent problems, the assistant can store the object under his shirt, next to his chest, until it is time to place the article. Storing the article under the arm is not good because of the chemicals in deodorant.

Work at this level until the dog leads you to the assistant without hesitation. It is important to practice this problem in all kinds of weather because this is the only way that you and the dog can learn how scent works in different weather conditions. Do not move on to the next level until the dog has made the association that the scent article identifies the person he is to look for.

Problems

The dog may become distracted and leave the assistant's path. If this happens, it is usually because the dog does not have enough drive to find people. Be sure to keep the distance and time lapse between the assistant's leaving and the dog's following short enough to keep the dog excited.

If the dog loses interest, go back to Level 1, with you hiding instead of an assistant, gradually increasing the distance and time. Once the dog seems to be very excited about the hide-and-seek game, switch to having an assistant hide. If the dog remains interested in the training, move on to the next level. However, if after repeated attempts to get the dog interested in scent-specific work, he does not respond, consider that the dog may prefer to airscent. If the dog is not interested in finding people at all, he may not be SAR material. Some dogs will work very well in short problems in which the excitement is always high but will lose interest when there is a time lapse. These dogs are not SAR material.

Test: Level 2

The assistant will leave a scent article at the starting point. You will take the dog to the scent article, show it to him, and then give him the command to find the assistant.

Mark the path the same way that you did in the training sessions. The observer can tell if the dog is following the scent by the enthusiasm that the dog shows while following the path of the assistant.

The dog will follow the path of the assistant and lead you next to the assistant, thus identifying that the assistant is the person whose scent he was following.

Level 3: Identification

Goal: To give a strong "found-assistant" alert and to build the handler's confidence in the dog's search ability.

Target Skill: The dog will give a signal (alert) to indicate that the assistant is the person who left the scent article.

Method

This exercise is important in the event that the missing person is in a group of people so that you will know which person's scent the dog was following. At this point in training, the dog will already know the mechanics of the alert. For example, if the dog is required to sit quietly in front of the missing person, the dog must know how to do so before training.

Several methods work well. One method requires that the assistant give the dog a special food reward. The food can be hidden on the assistant, and the dog is allowed to find the food after he gives the correct signal.

Another method is to give the dog the command for his alert (such as *sit* or *speak*) as soon as the dog reaches the assistant. If you like the bark alert, be aware that a barking dog might frighten a missing person. Whatever the alert, the dog must know how to do it on command before this level of training. Clicker training works well in this case. As soon as the dog looks at, touches, or otherwise acknowledges the assistant, you can give the dog a click. You will continue to shape the dog's alert in this manner until he gives the desired signal. The click will also reinforce that the dog did the right thing by going to the assistant. Of course, that's just a very basic look at how clicker training works.

Set up the problem in all weather and terrain conditions. First, the assistant leaves a scent article and hides about 150 feet from the starting point. He will make his path twist and turn, using wide sweeps, and will mark the path for you to see but so it's not noticeable to the dog. Note that by this time, the dog will be able to follow a scent path. Gradually increase the length of the trail, the amount of time that elapses after the assistant leaves, and the number of turns as you practice the exercise over a number of weeks or months.

You will lead the dog to the scent article and then give him the commands to look and to follow the scent. The dog will enthusiastically lead you to the assistant and give a found alert.

If need be, the dog can see the assistant leave. Once the assistant is in place, you will approach the starting point. However, you will take care that the assistant's path is not always a straight line in front of the dog. The scent is aged for between fifteen and thirty minutes.

It is important to watch the dog carefully to make sure that the problem is not too easy too many times. Otherwise, the dog could become bored and not want to do the work. The exercises must be interesting and challenging to the dog. This is a judgment call made by you, the assistant, and the observer. Each dog is different, and the dog's experience and age will influence quite a bit how you set up the exercises.

Problems

Sometimes the dog will be so excited about finding the assistant that he will not hear you give the command for the alert or he will not be able to control himself right away. If eiher of these things happens, wait for a second, let the assistant give the dog a quick reward or acknowledgement, and then have the dog give the alert.

Never correct a dog or withhold the reward from a dog who shows a high level of enthusiasm and excitement about doing the job. The goal is to build excitement, not curtail it. As the dog practices more, he will be able to give the alert.

Test: Level 3

Conduct this test in any weather and on any terrain features, using a scent trail of 150 feet long that has been aged for thirty minutes. The path will have some turns and will not be in front of the dog as he approaches the starting point. The dog will be eager to follow the scent of the assistant, lead you to the assistant, and then give an alert.

Level 4: Tougher Trail Problem

Goal: To solidify that the dog follows the path of an assistant based entirely on the scent.

Target Skill: The dog will follow a scent path when he does not see the assistant leave.

Method

Keep the dog away from the area while the problem is being set up. The assistant will drop a scent article and walk 150–200 yards away, leaving a scent trail that is not in a straight line. The scent trail will be aged for up to thirty minutes.

You will bring the dog to the scent article, show the dog the article, and then give the dog the *find* command. The dog will follow the scent path and lead you to the assistant, giving an alert.

At this point in training, lead the dog to the start of the problem from various directions. Bringing the dog to the scent article from different directions will help him learn to cast for a scent, which means to circle the object to find the correct path. If the dog does not do this, you can encourage him to look for the path. However, the path must be marked so that you can see that the dog always finds the right direction. This will assure you that the dog is able to determine the direction of the scent path on his own.

Problems

The dog, in his enthusiasm, may overshoot the correct path. If this happens, give the dog a chance to work it out on his own. If the dog consistently runs ahead and does not follow the scent path, it could mean that he is not using his nose to find the assistant. This happens when the dog is used to the problem being set up the same way time after time, so he expects the assistant to be in a specific place or to have taken a certain direction.

If the training area available to you is limited, there may be little variation in how the problem is set up. It may be necessary to change training locations so that you can set up the problem differently and the dog will not know what to expect. This will force the dog to use his nose.

If the dog's not following the scent path is an intermittent problem, it is most likely that the scent is not behaving in the manner that you expect it to. The dog could be following scent that drifted off the scent path. The way to test for this is to bring the dog to the scent path from different directions and see if the dog can consistently find the assistant.

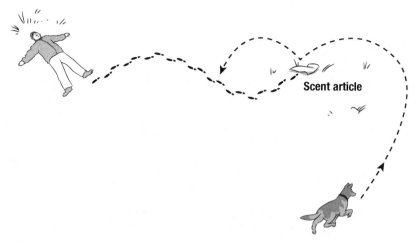

Casting for a track: the dog should be taken to the scent article and allowed to circle the article, if he wishes, to look for the trail. The trail should not always be straight ahead from the dog.

Test: Level 4

The assistant will lay a scent path for the dog, leaving a scent article at the start. The dog will not see the assistant leave, and the scent path will be aged for at least thirty minutes.

You will bring the dog to the starting point and give him the command to find the assistant. The dog should cast, pick up the right trail, lead you to the assistant, and give the alert.

Level 5: Using a Scent Pad, Not a Scent Article

Goal: To teach the dog to find a scent path without a scent article.
Target Skill: The dog will demonstrate that the identifying scent can be on the ground, not just on an article.

Method

The assistant will follow the same method as in Level 4 except that he will make a "scent pad," which means scuffing up the soil instead of leaving a scent article. The beginning of the path is clearly marked; however, you must be careful that the dog does not detect the marker and assume that it is the scent article. One way to mark the path is to hang bits of toilet tissue (biodegradable) or flagging tape at your eye level.

You will lead the dog to the starting point and allow him to determine the direction of the scent path. The dog will lead you to the assistant and give the alert.

Problems

The dog may be confused when there is no solid scent article. If the dog seems to be looking for a scent article, give the dog the *look* or *take scent* command while pointing to the scuff marks on the

A scent-specific dog can become so engrossed in following scent that he ignores his handler.

ground. By this point in training, the dog will understand that he is to follow the scent on the ground.

Test: Level 5

The assistant will lay a scent path without leaving an article for the dog to follow. You and the dog will not watch the assistant set up the problem. You will lead the dog to the scent path and allow him to cast for the trail; the dog should then lead you to the assistant and give an alert.

Level 6: Aged Scent Path

Goal: To build the dog's experience and to have the handler learn to work with the dog as a team.

Target Skill: The dog's scent-discrimination skills will be enhanced by working in situations that simulate actual search conditions.

Method

By the time the dog reaches this level of training, he will be proficient in the mechanics of scent discrimination. The purpose of this phase of training is to give the dog the opportunity to practice what he has learned and experience various field conditions. It is best at the beginning of this level that the weather conditions are favorable to help the dog succeed. As the dog gains experience, the conditions can become more difficult. However, still work the dog on uncontaminated scent paths in wilderness/wooded/field conditions.

The assistant will leave a scent path either with or without a scent article at the start of the scent path. The dog will not see the assistant leave, but the scent trail will be marked for you.

You will bring the dog to the start of the scent path and give him the command to search. The dog will follow the path, lead

Note: A scent path that is older than fifteen minutes will have scent drift or spillover; how much will depend upon the weather. An hour-old scent path will also have a different scent picture. Therefore, this part of the dog's training will closely resemble actual search situations. You must remember to let the dog put his nose where he feels it needs to be.

The assistant marks the scent path so that you can judge how much drift has taken place based on how the dog works. This is an important lesson for you in learning to read your dog. You will also learn more about how weather conditions affect scent.

you to the assistant, and give the alert.

As the dog progresses, increase the length and age of the scent path and the number of turns, one element at a time, until the problem is a mile long and twelve hours old.

This level of training requires planning and logistics to make it work well. With aged scent paths, the assistant may have to lay the scent path the day before training. One way to accomplish this without adding more of the assistant's scent to the area is to drive the assistant to or from the start or ending point. For example, if the assistant is driven to the starting point of the problem, the end of the scent path will be located in such a way that the

assistant can get in a vehicle to leave. When the dog runs the problem, the assistant drives back to the end of the scent path and hides for the dog.

Again, you and the assistant must consider how the weather could compromise the problem for the dog.

Problems

As the training problem becomes more difficult and the scent path is aged longer, you and the assistant have less control over the effects of the weather on the scent path and whether or not other people or animals enter the training area. For this reason, never correct a dog for what appear to be mistakes, such as missing a turn and then recapturing the trail. You must be able to recognize what is going on and assist the dog when needed.

If you feel that the dog is not able to complete the exercise, go back to a more controlled level to see if the dog himself is having a problem or if the problem lies with the training conditions. By this point in training, you must have faith in your dog and look at other reasons for failure, such as error on your part or the weather.

Test: Level 6

The assistant will lay a scent path, either with or without a scent article at the start. The problem will be 3/4–1 mile long and up to twelve hours old. It is important to transport the assistant to the end of the scent path before the dog starts the problem. The assistant will not walk over or cross the scent path that he created earlier.

A good scent dog will take his handler right to the missing person if he picks up the air-borne scent before reaching the end of the scent trail.

The dog is taken to the start of the scent path and allowed to cast to find the direction of the scent trail. He will lead you to the assistant and give an alert. Remember, at this point, weather conditions need to be favorable for the dog to succeed. For example, it is not a good idea to start the problem during the heat of a summer day. After the dog has more experience, he can work through more difficult problems, such as following scent in unfavorable conditions, to practice his skills and so you can see what he can do.

Level 7: Complicated Scent Path

Goal: To teach the dog that scent paths are not always easy.

Target Skills: The dog will have more "real" experiences and the handler will learn more about how the dog works.

Method

The assistant will lay a scent path as in Level 6, but now adding loops, backtracks, and turns. At this stage of training, the assistant will add to the scent path gradually by walking over streams and through water, climbing on large objects (such as rocks), and even ending the scent path high up in a tree or on another elevated obstacle. The dog needs to experience that the end of the scent path could be above him. The assistant will mark the path so that you can see how the dog works the problem each time.

Problems

The only problems that the dog might have are his lack of experience in handling the difficulties of the scent path, micromanaging by you, or error on your part. Remember, a handler who micromanages his dog tries to tell the dog how to do everything instead of letting the dog work the problem using his nose and experience.

Always give the dog the opportunity to work problems through, as micromanaging will hinder the dog's ability to solve problems. A handler who micromanages typically does not trust his dog.

Remember to always consider how the weather could affect the scent. Sometimes it is not possible for a dog to detect scent, no matter how good he is. This is the point in training when you will start to realize the dog's scenting limitations and how to assist the dog in finding scent.

Test: Level 7

The assistant lays a scent path up to 1 mile long and up to twelve hours old in fair weather conditions. The scent path will have loops, backtracks, turns, and breaks in it.

The dog is taken to the start of the problem; he will lead you to the assistant and give an alert. The observer will be watching carefully to see if you try to micromanage the dog or otherwise cue him as to where the scent path is located.

Level 8: Contaminated Scent Path

Goal: To teach the dog that a scent path may have two human scents and to follow the correct one.
Target Skill: The dog will learn how to distinguish between two different human scents.

Method

Assistant 1 leaves a scent article at the start of the scent path. The path is of a reasonable length and age, but is not too difficult for the dog. Assistant 2, not related to Assistant 1, will cross the path of Assistant 1. The reason why the two helpers cannot be related is that people have two major identifying scents: their own unique scent and their family scent. Therefore, to make the problem clear for the dog, do not pick two assistants who are related or who live in the same household.

Assistant 2 does not start at the problem's starting point, but crosses the path at a right angle, if possible, at least a quarter of the way down the trail. The point in the primary scent path where Assistant 2 crosses should vary from problem to problem so that the dog does not anticipate where the second path will be.

Assistant 2 marks the place in the scent path where he crossed it and then continues to an ending location far enough away from Assistant 1's ending point so that the dog will not think that the two assistants are together.

You will scent the dog on Assistant 1's scent article. When the dog encounters the spot where the paths cross, you will pay careful attention to the way the dog acts. If the dog starts to follow the wrong scent, let him go for a short distance in case the correct scent drifted onto Assistant 2's path. In most cases, the dog will correct himself within a few feet. If it becomes apparent that the dog is following the wrong scent, go back to where the two paths crossed and put the dog on the correct scent. At this point, you can give the dog the search command again.

Assistant 1 can leave a small scent pad (scuffed soil) just beyond the points where the paths intersect to assist the dog in choosing the correct trail. This is a good idea for the first few times that the dog practices this problem.

Once the dog gets the idea and can sort through simple scent contamination, use more than one assistant to contaminate the scent path. Vary the age of the primary and secondary scent paths until the dog can follow the correct scent path even if it is older than the contaminating scent path.

Eventually the scent paths can be side by side, having the correct scent path veer off at a specific point. Be sure to use traveled trails in meadows and woods. This type of problem will simulate a situation in which the missing person follows a path that other people have used and then leaves the path.

Once the dog can handle all of the aforementioned situations, the scent path can be left on various surfaces, such as in schoolyards, on playgrounds, and so on, that have not been heavily used for a few hours. Cooling down the area will allow the assistant's scent to be the freshest, yet the other scents will be there to contaminate the area. This will give the dog an opportunity to work in a real environment. The assistant will leave a scent path through these areas and then go to a less contaminated area so that the scent path varies in difficulty. One way to keep the dog excited and encouraged is to have the assistant leave scent pads periodically along the new and difficult surfaces until the dog is proficient at sorting things out.

Test: Level 8

This test involves three assistants—one will leave the scent article and the others will follow along for about half the length of the scent trail and then leave the path in two different directions. One of the secondary scent paths will be older than the primary path, and the other secondary path will be newer. One of the secondary assistants will leave the primary assistant's scent path at a quarter of the way down the path; the other will leave the primary path at halfway down the path.

After all of the scent paths have been aged for at least thirty minutes, take the dog to the starting point. The dog is given the scent article, and he will lead you to the correct person and give an alert.

Level 9: Aged Scent Path in Various Environments

Goal: To give the dog/handler team practice in different settings.

Target Skill: The dog will work out problems in different settings and the handler will have the opportunity to see how the dog works.

Urban search training in Holland.

Method

Up to this point, the dog has had light or no contamination on the scent path. Now the assistant will leave scent paths in heavily contaminated areas, such as shopping malls, school grounds, livestock yards, railroad tracks, and any other place that the dog may encounter on a real mission.

Include various indoor surfaces as well as outdoor situations. However, first make sure that the dog is comfortable with his footing on the various surfaces on which you want him to work. This may mean separate training sessions to accustom the dog to different surfaces. For example, if a dog becomes frightened on slick surfaces, he may not want to work on them again.

Always start with a "hot," or fresh, scent path in a new area. As the dog succeeds, age the scent path. It is OK to work to the point where he cannot find the scent path so that you will understand the dog's limits. It's important for a handler to know

his dog's limits so that he can determine whether or not his dog can handle a particular search mission. For example, if a handler knows that his dog does not do well in snow, he will be able to determine his team's effectiveness if called to search in snow. However, never stop a dog from trying on a real mission because it is impossible to know how much scent is available and what conditions will work for the dog.

Problems

The dog may become distracted at first when taken to public places. Try to avoid letting people pet or otherwise make a fuss over the dog so that the dog will learn that these places, which he may associate with social time, can also be work areas. If necessary, work the dog in these areas when there are no people present until he learns that they can be work sites.

Test: Level 9

Conduct the test in a heavily contaminated area, such as a shopping mall. It is not necessary that shoppers be present, but the area must have had people in it within the two hours before training.

The assistant lays a scent path through the area that is up to a half mile long and aged for one to six hours. The assistant will be at the end of the scent path when the dog works the problem.

Take the dog to the starting point and show or give him the scent article. The dog will lead you to the assistant and give the alert.

CHAPTER 11

BACKTRACKING METHOD

Robert J. Noziska of the United States Border Patrol successfully taught his dog to backtrack in 2001 and has been using dogs in this capacity successfully since that time. Backtracking is when a dog is given a scent to follow, but instead of following the scent path from the older scent to the new, fresher scent, he is taught to follow the scent from the new to the old, or backtrack.

This is a useful tool to use when one person has left a group of lost people to seek help, and the rescue team has to retrace the person's path to find the rest of the group. It is also useful in cases where a handler wishes to retrace a person's path to find clues and evidence.

A handler must teach his dog a separate command for backtracking. Otherwise, the dog will not know in which direction to go when encountering a scent path on a mission.

Level 1: Introduce Backtracking

Goal: To introduce a new concept to the dog.

Target Skill: The dog will follow a scent path from the newest or freshest scent to the oldest.

Method

Begin by having an assistant create a scent path that is long enough so that the dog cannot see the end of it. The length of the path will be determined by the geographic features of the training area. It should be long enough to be interesting for the dog, but for the most part it should be a straight line. The emphasis of this exercise is to introduce a new concept, not to give the dog a difficult, long problem to solve.

Once the assistant finishes the scent path, he should drive back to the beginning of the scent path, where he will hide or otherwise appear to be resting, simulating an exhausted or unconscious lost person. You can decide if the assistant should leave a scent article or if you will scent the dog on a footprint. It is impor-

tant that the assistant who laid the scent path not be near the dog when the dog starts the problem and not walk back to the start of the scent path. The dog should find the assistant at the end of the problem and receive a big reward.

After the assistant has been placed at the beginning of the scent path, bring the dog to the end of the scent path (the freshest scent). The scent path is in front of the dog and begins where he is started so that the only option he has is to go from the freshest scent to the oldest scent.

Give the dog the command to follow the scent path and praise the dog as soon as he takes a few steps in the correct direction. You can use the same command that you would use for following a scent path old to new, or you can use a new command along with the familiar command and gradually wean the dog off the familiar command, eventually using only the new command when the dog is to backtrack.

Problems

Some dogs may become unsure that the handler wants them to backtrack. If that happens, either encourage and assure the dog, or start over with a scent path that is shorter. If the dog is clicker-trained, the handler can click the dog as soon as he looks in the correct direction. If the dog is not clicker-trained, enthusiastic praise will work.

Test: Level 1

An assistant will leave a scent path 1 mile long and aged for no more than twenty

Getting ready to run a scent path.

minutes. The dog will be started at the end of the scent path (the freshest scent) and commanded to follow the scent path to the beginning. The dog will follow the path to the waiting assistant.

Level 2: Solidify Backtracking

Goal: To increase the dog's understanding of backtracking by following a longer, older scent path.

Target Skill: The dog will follow a more complicated scent path.

Method

Follow the instructions for Level 1, but increase the length of the scent path by a half a mile. Age the scent path for thirty minutes.

Test: Level 2

Set up the test the same way as in Level 1, but increase the distance of the scent path by half a mile and age the scent path for thirty minutes.

Level 3: Introduce Finding the Scent Path

Goal: To show the dog that the scent path is not always in front of him and straight ahead.

Target Skill: The dog will complete a more difficult exercise with more complications added.

Method

Set up the problem in the same manner (distance and age) as in Level 2, but bring the dog to the scent path in a way that he comes upon the scent path at different angles instead of always being in front and so that he meets the scent path at the freshest scent. Be sure the dog approaches the scent path in such a way that he does not have the option of going straight toward the freshest scent. Give the dog the command to follow the scent path and let him work the problem.

Test: Level 3

Have the dog approach the scent path at a right angle to the scent path. The dog will follow the scent path to its conclusion.

Level 4: Casting for the Scent Path

Goal: To teach the dog to cast for the scent path and choose the correct direction.
Target Skill: The dog will cast for the scent path.

Method

Have an assistant lay a scent path of the same length and age as in Level 3. Although you will know where the scent path begins, you will allow the dog to cast or "trail-locate" to find the scent path.

Allow the dog to choose which direction to travel. If the dog hesitates, encourage him to go from the new (freshest) to the old scent.

Test: Level 4

Have an assistant leave the same type of scent path as in Level 3. You will start the dog at least 300 feet away from the start of the scent path, and the dog will cast or trail-locate to find the scent path. When the dog finds the scent path, he will continue to follow the scent path from newest to oldest scent.

Level 5: Finding Clues, Not Humans

Goal: To teach the dog that there may not be humans at the end of the scent path.
Target Skill: The dog will find clues and evidence along the scent path.

Method

Have an assistant leave a scent path as in Level 4, and drop various articles, such as a wallet, starter pistol, or a dummy credit card, along the path. Bring the dog to the start of the scent path (freshest scent) and give the dog the command to follow the scent path. When the dog encounters the clues, praise the dog and let him continue along the scent path until he reaches the end. At the end, have a large piece of clothing for the dog to find.

Test: Level 5

Have an assistant leave a scent path as in Level 4 with no less than three clues for the dog to find. The handler will know what clues are left and approximately

A search team on the trail.

where they are located. The dog will find at least two of three clues. The alert signal for a clue will have been previously taught to the dog.

Level 6: Cast for the Scent Path and Find Clues

Goal: To test all of the previous levels of backtracking.
Target Skill: The dog will follow the scent path and find the clues.

Method

The assistant will leave a scent path that is approximately 2 miles long and aged for at least one hour, and will leave various clues along the scent path—no less than five clues and no more than ten. The clues will vary in size from shell casing to articles of clothing. You will allow the dog to cast or trail-locate to find the start of the problem and then lead you to the end of the scent trail.

Test: Level 6

The test problem will be set up as described in the Level 6 method. There will be five to ten objects or clues left along the scent path, and you will not know how many there are. The dog should find all of the clues.

Level 7: Ignore Clues

Goal: To teach the dog to ignore clues on command along the scent path.
Target Skill: The dog will respond appropriately to your signal that, in some instances, he is not to alert on clues.

Method

Arrange for a group of six people to assist with this problem. One person will lay the scent path and the other five will stay at the end of the scent path. However, prior to having the person lay the scent path of at least 2 miles long, have one individual from the group gather articles from the other members of the group. Each person will place his article in a brown paper lunch bag. The person who is laying the scent path will take the bags and dump the articles, one at a time, along the scent path. The person laying the scent path will not leave an article of his own.

When the person who is laying the scent path completes the path, he will be taken away in a vehicle to a location other than the beginning of the scent path, where the rest of the group has remained. The scent path is aged for at least two hours.

Scent the dog on the scent of the person who laid the scent path. Allow the dog to cast for the scent path and begin to follow it. When and if the dog hits on a clue, give the command *move on* in a non-emotional tone of voice. *Do not* recommend the dog to follow the scent path! You cannot be certain that another scent is not present, and you could be telling the dog to follow a totally different person's scent. As soon as the dog looks at the clue, quickly pick it up and encourage the dog to continue with the *move on* command. The dog will understand that he is to ignore clues.

Level 8: Practice

At this point, you will arrange for various problems to simulate the types of missions that you and your dog are likely to encounter. The scent paths will increase in length and age to the point where the

Note: In a case where a large group of people is lost, there could be so many clues left along the path that you may not want the dog to alert on clues, as it will slow him down. Even though the dog was scented on one person's scent, that scent may have drifted onto the clues left by the others in the party, causing the dog to "hit" on many clues. The *move on* command lets the dog know that the situation has changed. You would also use *move on* if you initially send the dog on a "find clue" scent path and it becomes evident that hitting on clues is not what is needed.

dog has difficulty. This will give the dog a chance to work out the problems and give you a chance to learn the limits of your dog. If the dog should fail to solve a problem, you will set up a shorter, easier problem for him to solve as soon as the two of you return to base.

Level 9: Clues or No Clues

This concept takes time and effort on your part and works best with younger dogs that have not been ingrained with one method of scentwork, but more experienced dogs are capable of learning it.

Goal: To establish a command that tells the dog at the beginning of each trail whether he is to find clues or not. This is helpful when the situation is to find clues and not people, or vice versa. **Target Skill:** The dog will understand what he should do before starting the trail.

Method

Begin by making sure that the dog understands the *move on* command thoroughly before starting this level of training. The method for teaching this command is relatively simple. Have the person laying the scent path leave other people's clues along the trail. At the start of the trail, add a command to the already established command that tells the dog to follow a specific scent. For example, if the command to follow scent is *track*, add something like *no clue* to the command. So, in this instance, there will be two commands at the same time: *track/no clue*. If the dog comes to a clue and slows down to investigate it, give him the *move on* command. By doing this repetitiously with short scent paths, the dog will make the connection that *track/no clue* means to ignore the clues along the scent path. For some dogs, it may be necessary to give the *no clue* command a few times during the problem. This is OK.

Once the dog gets this concept, you must alternate when you have the dog alert on clues and when you have the dog ignore the clues. If you fail to do this, the dog could generalize and not alert on clues at all.

For those readers who question whether or not a dog can make the distinction between a *track/clue* command and a *track/no clue* command, it is not much different than giving a dog any other commands, such as *down/stay*, *sit/stay*, or *stand/stay*. These also are two commands given together to tell the dog to do two things at the same time.

Test: Level 9

Have a person leave a scent path that is 2–3 miles long and drop other people's clues along the path. Depending upon the weather, age the scent path for two or more hours to allow time for the scent of the person who laid the path to drift onto the clues. Send the dog on the scent path with the command to ignore clues.

CHAPTER 12

WATER SEARCH TRAINING

As unpleasant as it is to think of the aspect of SAR that involves finding missing people who are suspected to be deceased, it is important. By finding a deceased person, the SAR team brings closure to the person's loved ones. In some cases there are also legal reasons, such as allowing the family to settle the estate.

Water search training will sometimes require more detective work than searching on land because it is impossible to see what is going on under the water. Sometimes a handler cannot determine what direction the current is flowing below the surface of the water or even if there is a current. Divers must search by "feel," and dog handlers must rely almost entirely on their dogs.

The scent from a body in the water will float upward via microscopic bubbles (the gasses and oils released by the body) and are carried by the

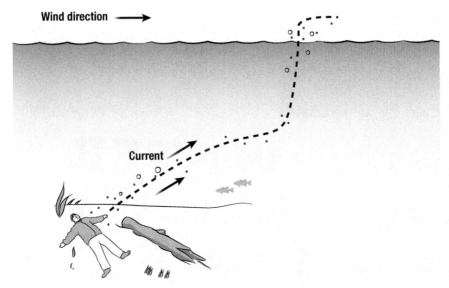

Wind direction ⟶

Current

The scent rises from the body and is carried with the current until it reaches the surface of the water, where the wind will carry it farther. Based on the dog's alerts, currents, wind, and weather, you must determine where the body will most likely be located to help the divers find the body.

water current away from the scent source. When the scent reaches the water surface, the air currents will carry it, sometimes in another direction.

Scent in water can collect on objects such as a log or the supports of a bridge. If the object sticks out of the water, the scent can travel up to the water surface.

Water can be different temperatures at different depths, causing thermoclines. A thermocline is the transition layer between the mixed layer at the surface and the deep-water layer; these layers are based on temperature. Sometimes the pressure caused by the thermoclines will prevent scent from rising or will force the scent to travel along the thermocline until it reaches a weak spot or break, where it

will continue to ascend. Sometimes the scent can travel along a thermocline and not break through until it is quite a distance from the scent source. Often the strength of the current or lack of a current will determine how the scent reacts to a thermocline.

Because ice is porous, dogs can detect human scent through ice if the conditions are right. Sometimes a dog handler may have to drill holes in the ice to help the scent escape. But keep in mind that the location of the scent is not necessarily the same as the location of the body.

Knowing some facts about human bodies in water will help with this type of searching. As the missing person is washed along the waterway, some skin may be removed from the body and cling to underwater debris. If the body is trapped, marine life and debris can damage the body, causing skin to be washed away and possibly caught farther downstream. This situation can occur if the body is trapped in the maytag or dynamics of a dam. This is when the body is caught in the circling water at the bottom of a dam; this causes the body to be pushed to the bottom and then forced to the top, circling around and around. A body can get caught when debris collects and acts like a strainer or blocks the flow of water like a dam. Often the clothes will be torn from the body and could get caught a distance from the body or continue downstream.

Initially, when a person drowns, the body will sink to the bottom of the water. Later, depending upon the water temperature and gas formation, the body may surface. Whether or not the body surfaces will depend mostly on the buoyancy of the body: positive (will float), negative (will not float), or neutral (will float, but not to the surface).

If the body is going to float, generally it will surface within two or three days in the summer, but it may take weeks or months in the winter. In some bodies of water that stay cold all year, such as the Great Lakes, the remains may never surface because the bodies do not bloat as they do in warmer water.

When the body is only partly submerged, the scent is usually carried in more than one direction by the current of the water and the direction of the wind. If a body is in a marshy/swampy area with a slight current and spilling into a pond or collecting in a larger area, the scent can saturate the entire body of water, causing dogs to give multiple alerts without being able to pinpoint the source.

To add another wrinkle to searching near water, scent from a body that is on land but near water can drift onto the water surface, causing dogs that are working from a boat to give an alert, even though the scent source is not in the water.

Dogs can and do find bodies in swift water with strong currents. They have also pinpointed bodies in situations where the scent has been taken north by the current and then south by the wind after reaching the surface. Never underestimate what a dog can detect with a handler who has proper training and is able to understand the conditions in which the dog must search.

For dogs that are being cross-trained, the command for water body recovery is a different command than for land searching. This way, the dog will know by the command what type of search he is to do.

Level 1: Preparation for Water Training

Goal: To familiarize the dog with the feel of a boat.
Target Skill: The dog will learn how to enter and leave a boat safely.

The dog must learn how to travel in a boat safely.

Method

Even though the dive squad assigned to the search will provide the boat, it is a good idea for the dog to feel comfortable with all kinds of boats. In some situations, there may not be a dive squad, and the searcher will have to use whatever boat is available.

To get a dog used to boats, start with a flat-bottomed Jon boat, such as a rowboat, on land. Let the dog enter and leave the boat until he feels confident about being in the boat. The dog must feel comfortable with a number of sensations, such as the material that the boat is made of (fiberglass, metal, or wood), the movement of the boat, and the boat's smells and sounds.

When the dog is familiar with the boat, rock it gently with the dog in it, still on land. Teach the dog to sit quietly while the boat rocks. When the dog is comfortable with this, gently bang the side of the boat to simulate the boat hitting a dock.

As soon as the dog can handle these exercises on land, do them on calm water. The dog should enter and exit the boat via a dock as well as from the shore.

Once the dog is content with being in a boat on the water, take the dog for a ride in the boat, going slow and making easy turns. Use electric- and gas-powered motorboats as well as rowboats. To most dogs, riding in a boat is fun.

Allow the dog to hang over the side and move around in the boat as long as it is done in a quiet manner. Do not allow the dog to jump into the water at any time. However, sometimes it cannot be helped, so if the dog should jump into the water, practice how to get him back into the boat. One method is to grab the dog by the tail and the scruff of the neck while he is parallel with the boat and lift him back in. If the dog is wearing a nonrestrictive harness, you can lift him back in with the harness. Never try to pull a dog into a boat by a neck collar. If the dog's hind end goes down, he will sink. The only way a dog can stay afloat is if his body is relatively parallel to the surface of the water.

It is not recommended that you try to lean over the side of the boat to grab the dog from underneath. You could fall out of the boat or capsize the boat. A few practice sessions will help both you and the dog feel comfortable with retrieving the dog from the water.

Never let the dog swim or jump out of a boat on a search mission, especially in contaminated water. If the dog should fall into contaminated water, wash him with antibacterial soap and clean water as soon as possible. It is also a good idea to keep a canine ear-drying agent handy to help prevent ear infections as well as an eyewash to rinse the dog's eyes. A veterinarian can recommend good products.

The use of the all-clear signal is very helpful with water searches, especially because you have less information about the search conditions than you would on land. (See the discussion on the all-clear signal in Chapter 7.)

Level 2: Beginning Water Training

Goal: To teach the dog that a human can be in water.

Target Skill: The dog will alert on human scent that has reached the surface of the water.

Method

It is ideal to train the dog in airscent work before undertaking water body training. Because water body training cannot be done with a scent article, the dog must understand how to look for people without a scent article. This transition may be difficult for the dog that is trained in scent-specific work only because he has been taught to look for a particular scent from

Water training for Marcia Koenig and Coyote, with Deb Tirmenstein instructing. Working from the bow of the boat, Coyote has found scent.

a scent pad or article. For this reason, airscent work is best as a precursor for water body recovery training.

Often in a water body search, the identity of the person is unknown. This can happen when a person is fishing or swimming and a stranger sees the person fall overboard and not resurface. In addition, sometimes someone will find an empty boat or other objects and assume that a person is missing. It may take hours or days for the family or friends to file a missing-person report. This is why airscenting dogs that are fully trained in water body recovery are useful in drowning situations.

The main goal of this exercise is to show the dog that people can be under the surface of the water. This is a concept of which most dogs do not naturally have an understanding. Ideally, this training is done with a dive team or certified divers, never less than two divers. The best and safest situation is to have a total of four divers, two in the water and two on the shore.

It is critical to work out all of the details of the training with the divers before the problem is executed. A communication system must be set up so that the diver can let you know when he is ready, and you can tell the diver when to surface to reward the dog. This can be via a rope that goes from the shore team to the diver or by underwater radio communication.

The diver will have a food reward that can get wet. Hot dogs work very well underwater and should be cut into pieces that can be easily handled by the diver.

Because some dogs get very apprehensive about the sight of a diver suited up with all of his gear, start by letting the dog watch the diver suit up, and then let the dog approach the diver and the gear. The diver can give the dog small pieces of hot dog as he suits up.

When the diver is ready to go into the water, allow the leashed dog to watch the diver wade knee-deep into the water. Encourage the dog to watch the diver in the same manner as in the beginning runaway problem. When the diver is out of sight, completely submerged in the water, put the dog into a boat. Have the boat zigzag in the direction of the diver; in essence, you're using the boat to range or quarter for the dog. If it is not possible for the dog to enter a boat in a timely fashion, the dog can watch the diver disappear from a boat nearby, and then the boat will zigzag as described.

It is best to do this problem on a still day without a breeze and in water without a current. However, if that is not possible, the breeze should be gentle, and any water current should be traveling from the diver toward the dog. As soon as the dog alerts on the diver, the diver surfaces and gives the dog the treat.

It is important that the diver reward the dog as soon as possible after the dog alerts on the diver. It is equally important for the boat to work far enough away from the diver for the dog to find the scent cone, but neither so far that it takes too much time nor so close that the scent

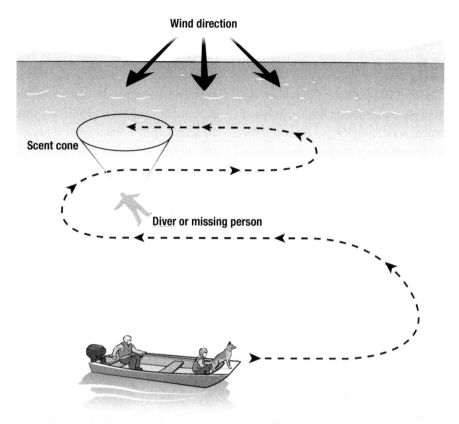

Wind direction

Scent cone

Diver or missing person

Grid pattern on water. It is important to use the same principles to grid a body of water as you would a section of land. If your boat has a motor, be sure that the fumes do not blow into the dog's face.

does not have time to reach the surface of the water.

Level 3: Working from the Shore

Goal: To look for bodies near the shore.
Target Skill: The dog will search from the shore for bodies in the water.

Method

When the dog understands that when he works from a boat, he is looking for people in the water, it is time to show him that he might have to look for people in the water from the shore. Keep in mind that up until this point in training, all land work meant that the missing person was on land. This fact has not gone unnoticed by the dog.

If possible, use a diver for this exercise. However, with care, an adventurous assistant can do the job. It is essential that all safety precautions are observed for all involved in the training, including the dog.

Select a body of water that is quiet and has a graduating sloped bottom, such as a lake or pond, even if it is very small. For everyone's safety, do not use a body of water that has sudden drops or gets deep quickly, such as a quarry.

Place the assistant about shoulder-deep in the water, hidden by weeds. Because the dog may go into the water and get very excited, the assistant can wear a face mask.

Start the dog downwind from the assistant and give the dog the command you will use for water searching. Note that some handlers like to use a differ-

ent command than the one they use for land cadaver searching (see Chapter 13), as it helps the dog understand that he is looking for a body in the water. Another possibility is to add a word to the cadaver command, identifying that the search will be water only. If necessary, guide the dog to work the shoreline. When the dog finds the assistant, the assistant will give the dog a treat (hot dog), and both you and the assistant will praise the dog.

Once the dog can handle this type of problem, the assistant can wear a snorkel or mask and float facedown in the water, ignoring the dog when the dog finds him. The dog will then perform the mechanics of the search/find by giving an alert and refind, leading you to him.

Susan Bulanda and Scout on a search with the Phoenixville Fire Department Canine SAR Unit and Phoenixville Fire Department Dive Squad.

Level 4: Multiple Boats

Goal: To reinforce the dog's concept that the missing person is in the water.
Target Skill: The dog will practice and will focus on the water, not on other people in boats and on the shore.

Method

Because each boat causes its own disturbance of the water and scent distribution, it is never a good idea for there to be more than one boat at a time on water searches. However, in some cases, it can happen. Often, the other boats and the people who are standing along the shore distract a dog. Therefore, it is a good idea to introduce this situation to the dog. Once the dog is comfortable working from a boat and consistently gives alerts on a diver or training scent, introduce more boats.

Start with other boats working as far away as possible but within your sight. It is OK if the dog notices the other boats but is not attracted to them. Gradually have the boats work closer to the dog. If the dog focuses on the other boats instead of looking for the diver, redirect the dog's attention to the water. If the dog continues to focus on the other boats, have the boats back off and go back to working with them at the point where the dog does not focus on them. Gradually bring the boats closer. It may take a few training sessions to accomplish the type of focus that the dog needs.

While it does not take a dog long to learn what water searching is all about, be careful that the dog does not give alerts on garbage. This is a tricky situation because the dog could find clues in the water, yet the dog must not give hits on old clothing or other such items that could be in the water but that do not have decomposition scent on them. A clue in the water would be the missing person's clothing, which has decomposition scent on it.

It is also a good idea to sink cadaver material in the water for the dog to find. Sigma-Aldrich is a life-science company that makes capsules that simulate the scent of a cadaver in water for training purposes. Water training scent can be the same material as used for cadaver training on land, placed in a net bag and weighted down in the water. Be aware that real cadaver material will contaminate the water.

Water work is stressful; depending on the search conditions, the dog may need to take breaks and frequent rests on shore. Sometimes the water may be contaminated, and you will not want him to get the water in his mouth, but no matter how hard you try to prevent it or how well trained a dog is, he may bite at and drink the water. Dogs do this because they taste the water and use the Jacobson's organ to assist them in locating the scent. If your dog does drink the water, he will have to relieve himself often; therefore, periodic shore breaks will be a necessity.

LEFT: Susan Bulanda and Scout, with the Phoenixville Fire Department Canine SAR Unit and Phoenixville Fire Department Dive Squad, on a mission to find two missing ice divers. RIGHT: Larry Bulanda and Ness make an ice find.

Level 5: Proofing the Dog

Goal: To build the handler's confidence in the dog and help the dog sort various scents.
Target Skill: The dog will locate human remains only.

Method

Once the dog has learned how to locate humans in the water, it is time to refine the dog's skills and help the dog sort through all of the different scents that may be in the water. Because no one knows for sure what could be in the water, you cannot control the level of scent contamination in the training environment. Therefore, a wise handler will create situations that allow his dog to experience different scents, much the same way that a handler will make land problems more difficult for the dog.

Give the dog problems in which the following are introduced (one at a time) to the training session:

- Clothing
- Dead animals
- Decaying vegetation, which produces methane gas
- Objects (for example, floating bottles, logs, and so on)
- Sewage
- Swamp gasses

Do not correct the dog for investigating these items, but do not allow him to alert on them or linger on their scent if you are certain that the target scent is not in the area.

Level 6: Learning to Work the Wind

Goal: To let the dog experience working the wind when confined to a boat.

Target Skill: The dog will work through simulations of actual search situations in different wind and water conditions.

Method

Set up training situations under each of the following conditions:

- The wind blowing in the same direction as the current, with the dog starting downwind from the scent source
- The wind and current traveling in the same direction, with the dog starting upwind from the scent source
- The wind and current traveling in opposite directions, with the dog starting upwind from the scent source
- The wind and current traveling in opposite directions, with the dog starting downwind from the scent source
- Feeder creeks entering the main body of water
- Top currents and undercurrents causing varying conditions

Dogs will work from the boat in various ways, depending on the type of boat. Ideally, a dog will work from the bow of the boat. It is not unusual for the dog to periodically lie down. If the dog hits a scent, he may change position and/or walk along the side of the boat. If the dog continues to the back of the boat, it may mean that the boat has passed the scent.

It is up to you to understand the dog's body language, because the dog may detect scent but not give an alert. The scent can behave on water the same as it does on land—it could loop, pool, and even settle in the bottom of the boat, causing the dog to give an alert or an indication through his body language.

Test: Level 6

Submerge a diver in at least 8 feet of quiet, still water. The diver can check if a current exists below the surface. The search sector will be no larger than 1 square acre. If an area of that size is not available, a long, narrow body of water will work. The test area must permit you and your dog to quarter (zigzag) enough to allow the dog to locate the scent on the water.

The dog will be enthusiastic about the search and show no fear of the boat, the water, or other people in the area. Once the dog finds the scent, he will demonstrate readable body language or if close to the source, an alert. The dog may paw or bite at the site where the scent exits the water, hang over the side of the boat, or give some other indication to point to where the scent is located. When the diver surfaces and rewards the dog by giving him a treat, the dog should be friendly to the diver.

CHAPTER 13

CADAVER TRAINING

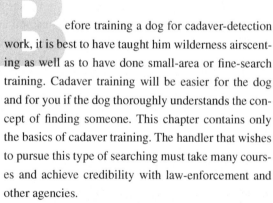

Before training a dog for cadaver-detection work, it is best to have taught him wilderness airscenting as well as to have done small-area or fine-search training. Cadaver training will be easier for the dog and for you if the dog thoroughly understands the concept of finding someone. This chapter contains only the basics of cadaver training. The handler that wishes to pursue this type of searching must take many courses and achieve credibility with law-enforcement and other agencies.

Cadaver searching can involve fine searching or may require the dog to range, as in wilderness airscenting. It depends on where the cadaver is located and how much of the body is involved in the search. (In SAR jargon, *cadaver* refers to any body parts or items used to simulate body parts, as well as the entire corpse.)

If the dog is cross-trained, you will have to give the dog a different command so that the dog knows he is going to look for a cadaver. Be sure that the word used is one that is appropriate to use around non-rescue personnel. It is wise to pick a word that cannot be connected with cadaver. Therefore, you do not want to tell the dog to look for the "stiff" or the "carcass." It could be a word such as *seek* or *look*, or a name of some type. The late Bill Tolhurst liked to use the Native America words *caha napoo*, which means "look for dead."

As discussed earlier in this book, we know that dogs are much more intelligent and aware than previously thought. Sight and scent both impact how a dog reacts to situations. A great new product line that simulates cadaver body parts is Soft-Tech™, made by Techline Technologies as part of their Techline Trauma Moulage and Appendages line. (See Appendix C for more information.) These simulated body parts are specifically made to last in the outdoors and are the same products used by various military and government agencies for their training. Handlers and units can scent them with cadaver scent for training dogs. The added bonus is that they prepare a handler for real-life encounters with cadavers, helping to eliminate critical incident stress. These products also help train the human searcher's eye to spot cadaver parts in the brush.

It is fortunate that since the first edition of *READY!* was published, an entire book has been written about cadaver-dog training. (See Appendix C for more information.)

Training Scent

Cadaver training can be difficult to set up because it is illegal in most states to possess body parts. This has forced handlers to use objects such as pig flesh, bloody human teeth, unwashed hair, fingernails, and bodily fluids such as can be found on gauze from surgeries, wounds, and so on. I do not recommend that handlers use pig parts at all or human hair alone. Dogs can tell the difference between pigs and humans, so pig parts do not provide the correct target scent for the dog. Hair does not decompose unless it has the roots, which include tissue matter, and will not provide the scent spectrum needed to teach the dog how to locate human remains.

There are two types of training scent: natural and chemical or artificial. Sigma-Aldrich produces a product called Sigma Pseudo™ Corpse, which is very successful in training cadaver dogs. They offer different levels of scent for cadaver training—Sigma Pseudo™ Corpse I for early detection and Sigma Pseudo™ Corpse II for post-putrefaction detection. Drowned Victim Scent is used for water body detection, and Sigma Pseudo™ Corpse Distressed Body Scent is used to train dogs for the detection of nonresponsive live bodies, such as in disaster training. Also available are Putrescine and Cadaverine (not manufactured by Sigma-Aldrich); however, these chemicals are extremely toxic and can be a health hazard to the dog and the handler, so it's best not

DEPRESSION IN DOGS

One of the most frequently asked questions by dog handlers and the public is whether dogs suffer from depression because of finding dead humans. It is has been my experience that they do not. In order for a dog to be depressed, he would have to associate death with the cadaver scent. While dogs are aware that something is either alive or dead, we do not know how dogs feel about death. From every indication, they do not view it in the same way that humans do. After all, dogs have no remorse for killing other animals. Dogs also often see dead animals in fields, by roadsides, and in other places and never show concern, even if it is another dead dog.

We teach the cadaver dog to find a scent, and he is rewarded for doing so. Therefore, as far as the dog is concerned, he is happy that he will get his reward. With this in mind, the question comes up, "What do dogs display that looks like depression?" This is easy to understand when the whole situation is considered. First, the handler could become depressed. The dog and handler are a team with a close bond, so it is easy for the dog to detect that the handler is not happy and react accordingly without understanding why. Another reason is that in disaster situations, where the dog/handler team works under extreme physical and mental stress, the dog could become exhausted. Often, handlers will overwork themselves and their dogs, causing sheer exhaustion. The dog could be both physically tired and reacting to the handler's emotions.

to use them. The Sigma products are much safer.

Natural materials consist of human flesh, human blood, bones (including teeth), and bodily fluids, such as pus from wounds, that can be used at any stage of decomposition. Keep in mind that decomposition occurs in five stages: fresh, bloat, putrefaction, liquefaction, and dry/skeletal.

Another good training material is soil from where a body has decomposed. This provides a wide range of scent for a dog. Adipocere (grave wax) is another excellent training aid. This gray, greasy substance forms on a body that decomposes in a wet environment.

A handler can also collect scent from vehicles involved in fatal accidents or that have bodily fluids from an accident. The scent is collected on gauze pads and stored in sterilized, sealed glass jars. Another source for scent is the soil from old graveyards or pauper fields where people have been buried in wooden coffins, but this can only be used with permission from legal authorities when circumstances permit. Although this works because the scent from a decomposing corpse leaks into the soil, it is not the best source of scent material.

All human scent sources must be stored in heavy glass or plastic containers and handled with surgical-quality gloves. (See the following section on storing training scent.) Never store scent materials in metal containers, as the containers will corrode.

All human material will contain bacteria and can transmit diseases. This means that all materials have to be handled carefully. The only way to preserve human material to prevent further decomposition is to freeze it. Soil samples should also be frozen. If the samples are older, the scent can be revived by adding a bit of moisture.

Storing Training Scent

I cannot stress enough that you must be very careful when handling and storing human materials. Use surgical-quality rubber gloves and plastic or heavy glass containers. Metal can react with the chemicals produced by decomposition, so do not use metal containers. Scent sources can be stored in jelly jars, double or very thick plastic freezer bags, or strong plastic containers. Remember that the containers will be frozen and/or refrigerated and transported. Therefore, they have to be substantial. It is a good idea to put the material in more than one container, such as a plastic bag placed inside a heavy glass or plastic jar. The outer container must be sealable and very secure to contain odors.

Training Containers

A variety of containers will work, depending upon where you plan to hide the material. The actual material can be placed on a gauze pad and the pad used as the scent source, or the material itself can be used. The scent must be placed in a container that will allow the scent to escape but will not allow the dog to ingest or otherwise touch the material. If the material is going to be buried for a period of time, it is essential that it be in a container that wild animals cannot open or drag away. It is also helpful to stretch a piece of nylon stocking over the opening of the container. This helps to keep soil out and prevents ants from entering the container and coating the source.

Some trainers like to use narcotics bags that are available through police-dog supply companies. Another easy-to-make container is a piece of 1- or 1$\frac{1}{2}$-inch PVC pipe about 6 inches long with PVC caps on each end. Drill holes in the pipe to allow the scent to escape. Be sure to wrap the scent source in gauze before placing it in the pipe.

Placing the Training Scent

In all cadaver-dog training, the placement of scent is important. Keep in mind that the dog can detect the scent of the person who hides the cadaver scent. Therefore, the person who places the scent source must contaminate the entire search area by walking though it instead of leaving a trail of scent that goes right to the hidden source; this will ensure that the dog learns to identify the cadaver scent. Dogs also notice that the ground is disturbed if the scent is buried. The disturbed soil will release its own collection of scents that are trapped underground, making the disturbed soil a clue.

The handler must consider all aspects that are involved in placing scent for training purposes. Never forget that the training container that the scent is put in will have its signature scent; thus, another precaution is to always use the same container for the training scent and have dummy containers of the same material that are never used with the training scent in them. This will proof the dog against using the scent of the container as a clue.

It is essential to consider all of the extra scents and conditions, varying them as much as possible so that the same extracurricular scents and visual characteristics are not always present in each training situation.

Cadaver Alert

The alert that the dog gives for cadaver searching must be one that is not damaging to the site or scent source. If the dog is cross-trained, the alert is one that is used for deceased people only. A convenient and reliable signal is to have the dog either sit or lie down next to the cadaver material. Never allow the dog to dig at

Three stills from crime-scene video footage of Madalyn Murray O'Hair's burial site. Mercy and Grace were handled by Vi Hummel-Carr Shaffer, DMORT; Xena (not pictured) was handled by Sue Hillard of the FBI. TOP: Mercy works the burial site. CENTER: Mercy alerts on the remains. BOTTOM: Grace turns into the scent while searching for the burial site. From video by Gene Henderson, forensic video/photography specialist for the Texas Department of Public Safety.

or touch the remains. Law-enforcement agencies are opposed to dogs that dig or touch the remains because it destroys the integrity of the scene.

When first introducing the dog to cadaver scent, you can watch for a natural alert that the dog gives consistently when finding cadaver scent. When you identify the dog's signal, you can enhance and reinforce it as the natural alert. Be sure also to teach the dog to give an all-clear signal to communicate to you when there is nothing in the area (see Chapter 7).

Level 1: Introducing the Cadaver Scent

Goal: To show the dog what the target scent is and imprint the scent in the dog's mind.
Target Skill: The dog will associate the scent with a name and reward.

Method

It is good to use some solid, stable containers, such as empty unused paint cans, cinder blocks with holes in the middle, identical plastic containers, a daisy wheel, or other similar objects, for this phase of training. Set up a row of three or four containers and put the cadaver scent in one of them. Always place the cadaver scent in a protective container inside the larger container. In each exercise, always use the same container for the scent so that the other

containers do not collect residual scent. This "hot" container should be stored in a different location than the "cold," or empty, containers.

Next, with the dog on leash, walk the dog up to the row of containers. As soon as the dog shows any interest in the container with the cadaver scent, give the command that you're going to use to identify cadaver and reward him immediately, as close to the target scent as possible. Timing the reward is critical so that the dog associates his behavior with the command and the scent. Reward the dog with whatever he likes or use a clicker. If using the clicker, give a click and then reward the dog. Be sure to click the dog at the first sign that he recognizes the scent.

Repeat this exercise, moving the containers around so that the hot one is always in a different position, until the dog will go to whichever container has the cadaver scent. If using food, hold the treat over the container as though the treat came from the source. If a ball or other object is the reward, have it "appear" over the source scent. It's important to note that if you're using chemical scent, make sure that the scent is present for the entire training session and does not fade away.

Repeat this phase of training for many training sessions. This phase of training is critical to developing the dog's commitment to finding the scent, which serves as the foundation for cadaver training.

Looking for evidence by sifting through soil from where a body was found. Members of King County Search Dogs assist forensic anthropologist Dr. Kathy Taylor (facing camera).

Problems

If the dog has been trained to find live people prior to cadaver training, and the dog shows aversion or no interest in the cadaver scent, you can try to associate the scent with a reward to communicate to the dog that this is a scent to identify. Some dogs do not like cadaver scent, so if after a number of sessions and attempts with different rewards, the dog still does not like cadaver scent, then this dog may not be suitable for cadaver training.

Test: Level 1

Place cadaver scent in one of six containers lined up in a row. Give the dog the command to find a cadaver, and he should lead you directly to the correct container.

Level 2: Adding the Alert

Goal: To create a reliable alert.
Target Skill: The handler will establish the alert signal with the dog.

Method

Once the dog consistently goes to the cadaver scent hidden in a container, add a pretrained alert to the training, as discussed in Chapter 7. As the dog goes to the correct container and acknowledges the target scent, add the chosen alert to the scenario. If the alert is to lie down, then as soon as the dog identifies the correct container, you will give the dog the

Members of Kittitas County Search Dogs search a yard for a possible body. Handler Dan Roberson and Gabby watch as Andy Rebmann probes where the dog showed interest.

down command and then reward the dog for lying down. Often, dogs will choose their own alerts—some will sit, some will stand, some will lie down, and so on. You can allow the dog to choose or you can teach the dog a specific alert.

Repeat this level until the dog will go to the correct container (target scent) and give the alert consistently.

Test

Have an assistant place a series of containers, one of which contains scent, in a small area. You will not know which container has the scent in it. Take the dog to the containers and give him the command to find cadaver material. The dog will correctly identify the container with the material in it.

Level 3: Teaching the Dog to Search for the Scent

Goal: To show the dog that cadaver is not always in a neat row of containers.
Target Skill: The dog will find cadaver scent in hidden containers in a larger area.

Method

At this phase of training, make the containers with the cadaver scent smaller than the paint cans/cinder blocks you've been using up to this point; hide them above ground in an area of about 20 square feet. You will start hiding the material in loose leaves, light brush, or grass.

With the wind blowing from the scent source to the dog, give the dog the command to look for a cadaver and let him range or search the area for the cadaver material. Once the dog finds the location, the dog will give the alert signal. If the dog has been airscent-trained and does a refind, you can ask him to do a *show me* after giving the alert. This way, if the dog is working an area and has a find but is not near you, he will lead you to the source. Eliminate the *show me* step if you want the dog to stay at the source to give an alert.

Problem

If the goal of the exercise is to do a fine search, the dog may want to rush through the area. If the dog knows a command for fine searching, you can use it with the command for cadaver searching. The dog is able to understand two concepts at once.

Sometimes a very enthusiastic dog will rush through a small area and then go back for a fine search. This is OK. If that does not work, you can walk the dog through the area and encourage him to sniff the ground while working in a grid pattern.

Test: Level 3

An assistant will place one scent source lightly hidden from sight in an area of about 30 square feet. You will give the dog the cadaver search command and, with the dog on leash, follow him to the scent source, where he will give the alert.

RIGHT: Grace, handled by Vi Hummel-Carr Shaffer, works a hay pile.

Level 4: Above-Ground Cadaver Search

> **Goal:** To make the search area more difficult for the dog.
> **Target Skill:** The dog will further develop his search skills.

Method

Hide the cadaver scent in an area covered with light brush and/or high grass or weeds at least 5 inches high. Be sure that the assistant (the person who hides the scent) has contaminated the area with his scent so that the dog will not trail directly to the scent. If you want less live scent around the cadaver material, the assistant can toss the cadaver material into the training area.

Once the material is in place, let the scent age for at least fifteen minutes so that a scent pool/cone can develop. If you want a larger scent cone, increase the delay time. It is important to increase the

LEFT: Andy Rebmann and Grizzly on a cadaver search.

delay time as the dog becomes more proficient in searching for a cadaver.

Next, send the dog on a search and let him lead you to the location of the scent. Once the dog has a find, he will give the alert and you will reward the dog.

Test: Level 4

An assistant will hide the cadaver scent in a situation to simulate a hidden body above ground. You will not know the exact location of the scent and will send the dog to locate it. Once the dog finds the scent, he should give the alert signal and refind the location if necessary.

Level 5: Underground Scent Source

Goal: To make it harder to find the scent, to have the dog use search strategies, and to show the dog that human scent can come from underground.

Target Skill: The dog will further develop his cadaver-search experience.

Method

Pick a training area with loose soil, such as vegetation matter, peat moss, and so on. Clay, mud, or other hard soil that does not allow the scent to rise is not good at this stage of training. Keep the weather conditions in mind when setting up this problem. If it is very cold (under 40 degrees F), the scent will not rise to the top of the soil as quickly as it will in warmer conditions.

Bury the cadaver scent under approximately 3 inches of soil. Do not pack the soil around the container, but leave it loose. Dig four or five dummy holes in the same area as the cadaver scent. Let the cadaver scent/material remain buried for a few hours to allow the scent to rise and allow the soil to settle a little bit. This way, the cadaver scent will intensify.

When it is time to train the dog, take him to the area and give the cadaver search command. Work the dog on leash if he cannot do a fine search off leash. Pay close attention to the dog's body language as he approaches the area with the hidden source. This will help you learn to read the dog before he makes the find.

Once the dog finds the cadaver source, he should give the cadaver alert and point to the location when given the *show me* command.

Once the dog masters cadaver sources hidden a few inches below the surface, make the hole deeper. Realize that the deeper the hole, the longer it must age.

Test: Level 5

An assistant will hide cadaver scent in a hole at least 10 inches deep in loose soil. Along with the scent-source hole, the assistant will create six dummy holes of the same depth with a few of these holes up to 10 feet away from the scent source. The area is aged for at least one to two hours. You will bring the dog to the area and give the command to find cadaver. The dog will find the correct hole, give an alert, and do a refind if necessary.

Level 6: Putting it All Together

Goal: To give the dog the complete picture.
Target Skill: The dog will work through exercises that simulate actual missions and will find a hanging cadaver.

Method

Once the dog is proficient and reliable in above-ground, buried, and submerged (water body searching) cadaver, it is time to put it all together for the dog. At this point in training, introduce the dog to the concept that cadaver scent could be up. Sometimes a hanging cadaver will present a tricky scent situation for the dog, as the scent may pool directly under the body, but the scent cone will be above the dog's nose level, creating a void at the level where the dog is trying to find the scent. There could also be a dead zone under a tree, with the scent collecting around the drip line of the tree branches.

Note: Follow this sequence for cadaver training:
1. Surface problems
2. Concealed problems
3. Shallow burial
4. Deeper burial
5. Hanging
6. Building and vehicle

If the dog knows how to wilderness-airscent, he will already understand that the person can be at a higher elevation. Nevertheless, it helps to reinforce this for the cadaver situation. Remember, the dog only learns what you show him. Therefore, the dog may not realize that a body could be in a tree.

When the dog reaches this level of training, you will also stage problems in vehicle junkyards, hiding the cadaver material under a seat, in a trunk, or somewhere else in a vehicle.

Use all types of training sites. The idea is to simulate mission situations. Be sure to place scent in rolled-up old rugs, under blankets, in leaf piles, under construction debris, and so on.

Level 7: Proofing the Dog

Proof the dog as described in Level 5 of Chapter 15, Disaster-Dog Training.

CHAPTER 14

AVALANCHE TRAINING

valanche searching is very dangerous. Only persons trained to work in avalanche conditions by recognized organizations should attempt it. The handler must know how to work in avalanche conditions first, and then the dog can be trained to assist.

The avalanche handler must be:

1. Near the areas where avalanches are a risk
2. Acclimated to the air at high altitudes
3. In the utmost physical condition
4. In possession of the correct equipment, including personal clothing and gear, because he has to spend hours and days in the worst mountain weather

Therefore, the dogs also must be hardy types who can withstand the weather and the physical demands of plowing through deep snow and climbing steep grades. There is always the risk of another avalanche triggered by the searchers themselves.

The concept for the dog is no different than with finding humans in any other situation. The main difference

is the level of urgency and the alert signal. The dog must work as quickly as possible and dig as soon as a scent source is located. Because of the very short time that a person can survive buried in snow, most avalanche finds are body recoveries.

Fortunately, since the first writing of this book, an entire book has been published about avalanche-dog training. (See Appendix C.)

Level 1: Preparing for Avalanche Training

Goal: To familiarize the dog with the available modes of transportation.
Target Skill: The dog will travel in a vehicle on snow.

Method
With safety foremost, introduce the dog to all of the modes of transportation available to ski-patrol personnel. This will include ski lifts, snowmobiles, and running alongside a person on skis. The dog has to practice getting onto and off of a ski lift until he can do this comfortably and without fear. It is also a good idea to familiarize the dog with a rappelling harness in the event that it is necessary to airlift the dog/handler team. Remember to always have a method of securing the dog while on or in snow vehicles.

The avalanche dog should first be trained in wilderness airscenting. It helps if the dog knows the concept of finding

Sue Purvis and Tasha, ready to search in the snowy mountains.

a person and giving an alert signal; it is then only a matter of teaching the dog a few new rules about searching in the snow.

Level 2: Finding an Assistant

Goal: To teach the dog that people could be under the snow.
Target Skill: The dog will learn to dig to find a person.

Method
Cover the assistant lightly in snow in an open area. Once the assistant is in place, bring the dog to the area and give the avalanche search command. Because the dog is already wilderness airscent-trained, he will naturally look for the missing person. The scent cone will make it obvious to the dog where the person is hiding. The dog will lead you to the hidden person and paw at the person; you then

LEFT and BELOW: Stacie Burkhardt and Jake of King County Search Dogs, Washington, training on a chair lift in Montana.

praise the dog for pawing and encourage the dog to dig.

Level 3: A Person Buried in Snow

Goal: To develop the dog's concept that people can be buried deeper in snow.

Target Skill: The dog will find an assistant buried deeper in snow.

Method

The assistant will sit in the snow, in a hole of a depth that allows his head and the top of his shoulders to be exposed. When the assistant is in place, you will start the dog from an area far enough away to allow him to search, giving him the *find* command. The dog will search the area and start to dig or otherwise try to get next to the assistant.

Avalanche dog Tasha works a site, looking for a missing person.

Level 4: The Completely Covered Person

Goal: To give the dog the experience of finding an assistant who is completely buried.

Target Skill: The dog's dig alert will be strengthened.

Method

Hide the assistant in a snow cave that either is open in front or has snow piled in front of it so that the dog cannot see the person. The dog will search and find the assistant. As the dog progresses through this level, increase the depth of the snow cave as well as how much the assistant is covered.

Test: Level 4

Set up a problem as outlined in Level 4, but the location of the assistant will be

Handler Patti Burnett and Magic do avalanche training at Monarch Ski Resort in Colorado.

unknown to you. The dog should quickly find the assistant and dig as an alert signal. The dog should not stop digging until he reaches the assistant.

Note: Observers or safety personnel who know where the assistant is hidden in the snow must be present in all training situations. The hidden assistant will have protective covering and a radio to call for help if needed. If the dog is cross-trained, the command for finding someone in snow is different from the commands for other types of searching. The handler, assistant, and other people involved in this type of training must understand the types of snow pack, how to build a snow cave, and cold-weather first aid.

Once the assistant is hidden, the dog is sent to search. Never keep an assistant buried in snow for a long period of time. Because this training is only done with a qualified avalanche/mountain rescue unit, all of the fine details are not covered in this book. The purpose of this chapter is to provide an overview of avalanche rescue.

Transporting an avalanche dog (Rottweiler) in Europe.

CHAPTER 15

DISASTER-DOG TRAINING

A n entire book is needed to cover live-person disaster training, and since the first writing of this book, one has been written. (See Appendix C.) This chapter will cover only the basics and concepts of disaster training.

Disaster-dog training is broken down into two disciplines: live-person rescue and deceased-person/remains recovery. There are differences in the search strategies and training that the dog/handler team must learn for rescue and recovery work. Many handlers, experts, and teams believe that teams trained for disaster or mass-fatality recovery should not work in the area of live-person disaster search situations.

Mass-Fatality Disaster Search

Searching for human remains or fragmented remains in a mass-fatality situation differs in many ways from conducting a search for live victims. Many dog units are experienced in live victim search and cross-train in other disciplines, including cadaver search. However, searching simultaneously or consecutively for live and deceased victims with the same cross-trained dogs can create major problems. One problem is that a dog that is not thoroughly proofed off everything except human remains has, in many instances, wasted the extrication technician's valuable time in dismantling a rubble pile because the dog alerted on things other than cadavers. This is not acceptable.

Mass-fatality searching requires proficiency in finding and pinpointing multiple human sources—either full-body or fragmented remains—in areas with large amounts of blood, bodily fluids, and heavy contaminants from other sources. Dogs are required to distinguish and alert on the actual remains amid the blood and other odors. A handler must be able to recognize and interpret his dog's alerts and body language, which may be very subtle. Mass-fatality searching also requires that the dog be thoroughly trained in the full spectrum of cadaver scent—fresh, old, burned, and so on.

To work in this environment requires a high degree of confidentiality and ethics because of the nature and specialization of cadaver search. For example, a handler must never take photos of human remains for any reason, including so-called "teaching" purposes.

In addition to the qualifications mentioned for disaster search for live victims, the cadaver-dog unit responding to a disaster must be proficient in all types of land searching; water searching; fire, building, and vehicle searching; grid searching; and hasty searching. The unit must be capable of working in wilderness, populated, and disaster environments, including working in the presence of other searchers, other individuals, and heavy equipment. In addition, clue awareness, crime-scene preservation, chain of custody, recovery, and health and safety practices are extremely essential.

For any type of disaster work (or any type of search work for that matter), an individual handler who is not associated with a unit or who is alone must never attempt to use a dog at a disaster site. Like avalanche searching, disaster work is very dangerous for both the dog and the handler. It takes a team effort for disaster searches to be successful. Except for small, isolated events, the cause of the disaster will present extra risks to the rescuers.

A disaster search can involve many different situations that use all aspects of SAR training. However, most people think of major disasters when they talk about disaster dogs.

Events such as terrorist attacks, bombings, hurricanes, earthquakes, and mudslides come to mind. Yet, on a smaller scale, an apartment-building or factory fire, a forest fire, a structurally unsound abandoned building, or an old barn that collapses can require the search skills of a dog/handler team trained in disaster work. Often these situations are not classified

Larry, Susan, Scout, and structural experts search in the aftermath of the 1994 Limerick, Pennsylvania, tornado.

as large-scale disasters, but the skills and training needed for safety still apply.

Handlers and other unit members who respond to disaster situations need special training in disciplines such as the dynamics of collapsed structures, hazardous-material handling, and confined-space extradition; most importantly, they need to be mentally able to handle the sights, sounds, and smells of a disaster. Some disaster situations are very similar to battlefields during wartime.

Disaster searches are often emotionally charged, capable of triggering very strong emotions in the rescue personnel, no matter how hard they try to control their feelings. What happens sometimes is that dogs and handlers who are trained to find live people go into a disaster situation with that in mind. When they do not find live people, but keep coming across deceased people, handlers may become very depressed and feel that their work was not a success. As a result, dogs can react to their handlers' depression. (See the section about depression in dogs in Chapter 13.)

The rescue/recovery person who responds to a disaster search must be able to be professional, to maintain a cool demeanor, and to make decisions based on search safety and logic, not on emotional issues. Be sure to read Chapter 20 (on search management).

Some individuals who respond to disaster situations have needed special counseling after the missions are over. There are special counselors for what is termed *critical incident stress debriefing*. The mental effects of disaster searching can affect a person at any time in his life, not just during or right after the incident. It is the same as post-traumatic stress disorder, which many military personnel experience.

Considerations

The scent cone at a disaster site does not behave in the same way as it does in wilderness searching. There is no way to predict how it will behave because the type of debris and the way it is piled will channel the scent. Wind and weather will also affect the scent, and so will the conditions or arrangement of the debris pile and the strong smells of contaminants (fire, water, dust, and so on) in the debris pile. This is especially true of large, collapsed buildings.

When training, it is helpful to set off smoke bombs, one at a time in various locations, after the exercises are over to see how the scent travels under those specific conditions. This will help you simulate a disaster site as closely as possible as you set up training problems for the dog. The goal is to allow the dog to learn how to work the drafts that come from the site. All of the elements at a disaster site will affect how the dog works.

The dog must be controllable off leash, trusted to work out of your sight, and able to take directional commands from a distance. Agility training for disaster work is essential and is discussed in more detail in Chapter 18.

As with all other types of searching, some dogs who work well on other types of missions will not work well in disaster situations. You must be honest about your dog's ability and desire to do this type of search work.

The chapter on additional commands is essential for disaster dogs, as is special training for the alert signal. The all-clear signal (see Chapter 7) is very useful for disaster work, such as in minor situations where a dog is asked to check an area that may or may not have a person trapped. When people think of disaster searching, they usually assume that there will be bodies present, but that is not always the case. Also, the dog must be proofed against food, dead animals, live animals, live workers, and clothing.

As mentioned previously, there is considerable debate over whether or not a dog can or should be cross-trained to find both live and dead victims in a disaster situation. A cross-trained dog would have to give a live person alert and a dead person alert. The main problem with having a dog give two different alerts is that there may be a live person in the rubble in the same area as the deceased person. The scent from the live person may be weaker than that of the deceased person, and the dog could possibly miss the live scent because he recognizes the cadaver scent, which is stronger. Keeping in mind that the dog will have to choose between

ABOVE and BELOW: Marcia Koenig and Coyote, searching after Hurricane Katrina in Pass Christian, Mississippi, in September 2005.

ABOVE and BELOW: Aerial photos of the search site after the Limerick, Pennsylvania, tornado in 1994.

POST-TRAINING AND POST-MISSION CARE

Each time the dog goes onto a rubble pile or enters any other site that contains debris, you'll need to examine him for injuries, cuts, and other physical problems afterward. This includes checking the dog's eyes, ears, fur, mouth, and feet, as well as an overall body check. It's necessary for handlers to take precautionary measures and be trained in canine first aid. Always assume that the dog has encountered toxic, noxious, and other types of hazardous materials. Realize, also, that using a dog on a real disaster mission could cause the dog to suffer long-term health issues and even death. Humans may have hazmat suits and masks to protect themselves, but dogs do not.

the two, or could give both alerts, his handler could be confused as to which one it is. If the handler sends the dog to search with a live body command, it could also cause confusion on the part of the dog as to which to alert on. Whether or not cross-training is successful depends on the handler's skills, the time put into training, and the individual dog.

The alert for live people must be a bark alert. For the most part, you will be close to the dog. For safety reasons, the dog does not do a refind or a retrieve alert, and he should not dig. Although some dogs will paw at the site of a trapped body, this is not the same as the aggressive digging that the avalanche dog is required to do. Note that for body recovery, gentle pawing at the site is a good alert. Because of the rubble, a *down* or *sit* may not be safe or possible.

The reward for the dog is not a game of tug or retrieve unless the dog understands that this is done off the rubble pile. A dog is capable of waiting for his reward, but it means that the dog must have a high work drive to sustain the enthusiasm needed for the delayed gratification.

Keep in mind that for safety reasons, the dog will work without a vest or collar. Therefore, the dog must be obedient and able to work this way. If your dog uses the vest and collar as a cue, you will have to develop a new cue to let him know what type of searching is in store.

The Training Site

Finding a disaster-training site is not always easy because it involves a lot of debris. While the site needs to simulate a real disaster, it must also be safe to work on, under, and around. Never forget that many of the people who will train on the site are not experienced disaster personnel, so it is essential for extra care to be taken to make the training safe. Special consideration must also be given when placing assistants at the training site. They must not be in a position where debris could fall on them or trap them.

The ideal site will have concrete rubble along with other materials. This is because most building collapses have reinforced concrete on site. Wooden pallets, boxes, bricks, pipes, logs, or abandoned buildings with debris in disarray will also work. The site has to contain enough debris so that the dog will have to practice his agility.

Level 1: Working Near a Disaster Site

Goal: To build the concept for the dog that people are hidden in debris.
Target Skill: To acclimate the dog to working around debris.

Method

If the dog is trained in wilderness search techniques, the transition to disaster work is a matter of introducing the circumstances to the dog, teaching the dog the correct alert, and fine-tuning the dog's agility and control. To start, be sure that the dog knows the commands and agility exercises in Chapter 18. At this level of training, it is important that the dog is not injured or frightened. If the dog is hurt or alarmed, he may hesitate to work around debris again.

The best way to begin this phase of training is to start with an assistant lying or crouching near debris, out in the open. The area around the assistant will be clear of anything that the dog could step on or otherwise wound or upset him.

The assistant will position himself without the dog watching. You will bring the dog to the site, give the disaster search command, and then let the dog find the assistant. If the dog does not know a disaster search command, you can do a few simple runaways with the dog while giving the new command. The dog will catch on quickly.

When the dog finds the assistant, you and the assistant will reward the dog. This level is repeated until the dog shows enthusiasm for the problem.

Problems

The dog may be nervous around debris and loud noise. If the dog does not gain confidence after a few training sessions, you should go back to agility work (see Chapter 18) and help the dog become comfortable around loud noise. If that does not give the dog confidence, then he may not be a good candidate for disaster work.

Level 2: Hidden Assistant

Goal: To introduce the concept to the dog that people may not be visible.
Target Skill: The dog's drive will be built and heightened.

Method

The assistant will hide out of the dog's sight, behind an object but not buried in debris. Bring the dog to the site and give him the command to find. The dog will search the area and find the assistant. Do not require the dog to climb on debris at this point in the training.

Do this scenario over a few training sessions with the following variations:

- The assistant will hide with you in sight; the dog will not see him hide.
- The assistant will hide so that the dog will lose sight of you to find him.
- The assistant will hide with you out of sight and in such a way that you will approach the assistant without the dog seeing you. The goal is for the dog to find the assistant with you out of sight and give the alert to indicate a find.

In each case, the dog stays with the assistant, giving a bark alert until you arrive.

Level 3: Hidden Assistant in a Box

Goal: To teach the dog that the assistant may not be accessible.

Target Skill: The dog will demonstrate drive and will stay with the inaccessible assistant.

Method

The assistant will have an object to hide in, such as a culvert, a box made for this purpose, a section of large piping, or another item that the assistant can fit into. The object will be at the rubble site but not in the debris, only near it. Do not require the dog to climb over rubble to do this problem.

This phase of training is done in three parts:

1. The assistant will hide in the object with the end of the object opened.
2. The assistant will hide in the object with the end of the object closed and will come out when found.
3. The assistant will hide in the object with the end closed and will not come out when found.

Once the dog readily finds and approaches the assistant hidden in the object with the end opened, gives an alert, and gets his reward, the exercise is repeated with the end of the object closed. When the dog barks and gets excited, the assistant opens the end and lets the dog come in to him. Once the dog accomplishes that, the exercise is repeated again, but this time the assistant will not open the object or acknowledge the dog. You will remove the dog and give the dog the reward. This will simulate a disaster situation in which the dog finds someone but other teams must extract the person while you and your dog continue to search for other people.

Disaster training in Holland.

Level 4: Hidden Assistant on a Rubble Pile

> **Goal:** To give the dog experience with finding people on a rubble pile.
> **Target Skill:** The dog's disaster-search concept will be reinforced and the dog will practice his problem-solving skills.

Method

This level of training will combine all of the previous training. In all cases, the dog will find the assistant and give the bark alert. You and the assistant will try to imagine all of the possible situations that the dog will encounter in a disaster situation. Following is a list of suggested training scenarios:

- The assistant is visible in the rubble pile (can be buried, but still visible).
- The assistant is visible but out of your sight.
- The assistant is visible, and you work off the rubble pile, directing the dog on the rubble pile.
- The assistant hides out of the dog's sight and is not visible. When the dog finds the assistant, the assistant rewards the dog.
- The assistant hides out of the dog's sight and is buried or not visible. When the dog makes the find, the assistant ignores him.

Level 5: Proofing the Dog

> **Goal:** To simulate real disaster situations.
> **Target Skill:** The dog will search while ignoring distractions.

Method

At this stage of training, the dog must clearly understand the "what and how" of searching for people in rubble and debris. The final phase of this training is to proof the dog. At this level, you will begin to work among the types of items (placed by the assistant) that are found in a disaster situation. You will decide what items to proof your dog against. They can include, but are not limited to:

- Bedding
- Cadaver material (if the dog is going to find live people only)
- Canine food
- Clothing
- Dead animals
- Dirty diapers
- Household items with human scent
- Human food
- Live animals
- Noise on site, construction equipment, jackhammers, etc.
- Sewage
- Workers on site

Combine the items for proofing the dog in one hole; sometimes spread them out in different holes. Be sure to place the items in the same hole as the assistant and in dummy holes. Proof the dog with different items and a combination of items during each training session so that the dog does not think that the items he encounters will always be the same.

For example, have the assistant hide with someone else's bedding. Then have a dummy hole with a live animal, such as a caged rodent, in it. Another dummy hole can have dog food and a used diaper in it. The point is to be inventive and create as many scenarios as possible.

Dog and handler being airlifted at a disaster site.

Handler Agnes and Seven, from the Dutch SAR unit, at a disaster certification test hosted by the Polish SAR team.

Keep in mind that in disaster searching, the dog alerts only on humans. If the dog is cross-trained, there will be one signal for live and one signal for cadaver. Otherwise, the dog will be trained for one or the other and have only one alert signal in this situation.

Level 6: Advanced Training–Live Person

> **Goal:** To complete the disaster-dog skills.
>
> **Target Skill:** The dog will practice all of the skills necessary to perform disaster searching.

Method

By this time, the dog will have learned all of the skills necessary to perform disaster searching. He must be able to:

• Find live humans only
• Maneuver rubble piles safely
• Take directional commands
• Work at a distance from you
• Give a strong alert
• Have the physical ability to perform the required tasks

Now is the time to introduce multiple assistants to the search problem. Up until this level, the dog has had one find for each problem. It is now time to teach the dog to keep searching for more people.

Have the dog find one person in the rubble pile. When the problem is completed, have a second concealed person, who is in a hole but not buried, stand up and wave a toy for the dog. You again give the dog the command to find and encourage the dog to go to the second person. This will teach the dog the concept that there can be two people in the rubble pile. If the dog is reluctant to leave the first assistant, have that assistant ignore the dog when the second one stands up.

As soon as the dog starts to go toward the second assistant, the assistant will duck back down into the hole. The handler rewards the dog when he finds the second assistant. Repeat this problem until the dog will find an unresponsive assistant and then go to the next unresponsive person. Depending on the dog, the handler can work up to more than two assistants on the rubble pile.

Level 7: Adding Directional Commands

Goal: To give the handler confidence in the dog when the dog is away from the handler.
Target Skill: The dog will practice working with directional commands.

Method

Once the dog has mastered all of the skills needed to perform a disaster search, it is necessary to practice them in a situation as close to an actual mission as possible. This last phase focuses on letting the dog work at a distance from you, taking directional commands. It is important that you are confident in the dog's ability to find and alert on assistants so that you can learn to trust the dog when he is at a distance.

You will have one or two assistants hide in the rubble pile. Take the dog to the base or outside of the pile and send him onto the pile to search. You will know where each assistant is located so that you can direct the dog toward the assistants. This way, the dog will also learn to trust your judgment. Once the dog works well, you will allow him to make the finds on his own, without direction. This is how dog and handler learn to become a team.

Level 8: Disaster-Dog Test–Live Person

Goal: To see how well the dog/handler team works together.
Target Skill: Teamwork and trust between dog and handler will be built and reinforced.

Method

An observer hides from one to three assistants in a rubble pile, and you will not know where they are. You and the dog perform a mock search to find the assistants. For clarity, mock searching simulates an actual mission from arrival time to departure time instead of focusing only on the dog's training. This includes incorporating any unit SOPs.

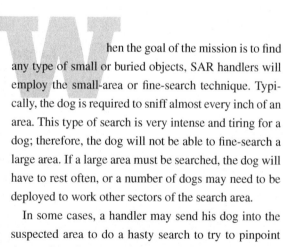

CHAPTER 16

SMALL-AREA OR FINE SEARCH

(ARTICLE, EVIDENCE, AND CADAVER)

When the goal of the mission is to find any type of small or buried objects, SAR handlers will employ the small-area or fine-search technique. Typically, the dog is required to sniff almost every inch of an area. This type of search is very intense and tiring for a dog; therefore, the dog will not be able to fine-search a large area. If a large area must be searched, the dog will have to rest often, or a number of dogs may need to be deployed to work other sectors of the search area.

In some cases, a handler may send his dog into the suspected area to do a hasty search to try to pinpoint the section that needs fine searching. If this method does not help narrow down the area, then the whole suspect area will be fine-searched.

The focus of this chapter is not to teach the dog what to find, but how to search under these circumstances.

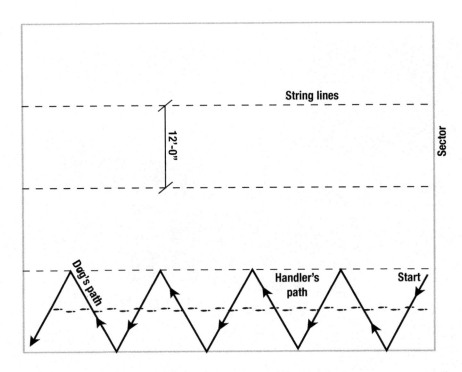

String lines

12'-0"

Sector

Dog's path

Handler's path

Start

Fine search with string lines. Dividing a small sector with string lines helps to show the dog that he is doing a fine search, and it also helps you identify where you need to search.

There are a couple of methods that work well for fine searching. String lines can be used to outline an area of about 12–24 square feet. Inside the marked area, additional string lines are set up about 12 feet apart and the length of the area. Handler and dog will walk each "lane" with the dog on leash, ranging back and forth in front of the handler.

Another way is to cross-grid an area. This is when the handler works from north to south, gridding the whole area. Then the team grids the same area from east to west. With the dog on a 6-foot leash, the dog will range about 12 feet across the handler.

Level 1: Teaching the Concept of a Fine or Small-Area Search

Goal: To teach the dog to work slowly and to methodically search the entire area.

Target Skill: To develop teamwork between the dog and handler and to teach the dog to slow down.

Method

It is best to set up this problem in very still weather conditions. The temperature

Dog performing a small-area search in a sector with string lines.

is not as critical as the wind. You must set up the problem so that the dog does not airscent the hidden object; rather, he needs to do a fine search to locate the object. The dog must know the *check* command, which tells him to search an area or spot that you indicate, usually by pointing to the spot.

Hide the object (either an article or cadaver scent) from plain view in the area. If it is buried just below the surface, a few dummy holes or areas of disturbed earth are also located throughout the area. Let the area cool off before sending the dog, because it is not a good idea to have other scent saturating the area.

String lines that section the area into grids will help the dog understand what is expected. The dog will notice the string lines and, as the training continues,

realize that they are boundaries.

There are two ways to command the dog: the first is to teach the dog a different search command that means to fine-search, and the second is to give the dog the regular search command and a *slow* or *easy* command. The new command or the addition of the *slow/easy* command will communicate to the dog to fine-search the area. If the dog is used to working off leash, the signal to the dog could be the *slow/easy* command combined with working on leash. If you have a very active dog that has trouble slowing down, refer to the *slow* command in Chapter 18.

At first, the dog may try to run ahead and rush. If the dog does this, simply stop and point to the ground, giving the dog the *check* command and the command to

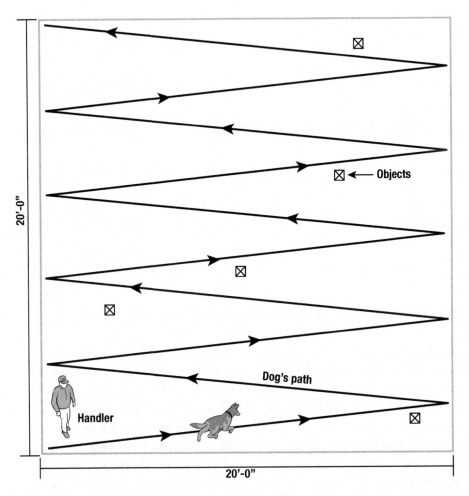

20'-0"

20'-0"

Objects

Dog's path

Handler

Small objects are randomly placed in the area. The handler will direct the dog to search the area using a grid technique.

fine-search. Be sure to only redirect the dog; do not correct the dog.

This will be a quick search. The dog must use a passive alert, such as to sit, lie down, or stand and bark to indicate where the object is located, for this type of searching. It will be a different alert than is used for other types of searching;

however, if the dog knows how to give a passive alert, this is acceptable. Some handlers like to add a bark to the passive alert. For the dog that is going to be a cadaver dog only, the handler can use this exercise to teach the dog how to perform a more precise search and to help a young dog learn to work slowly.

Level 2: Multiple Objects in One Area

Goal: To teach the dog the concept that there can be more than one item to find.

Target Skill: The dog's drive will be established and his understanding about this type of searching will be increased.

Method

The problem is set up the same way as in Level 1, except now there are two or three items hidden. As the dog becomes proficient in finding multiple items, add as many as you feel necessary for the type of mission in which you will use the fine-search technique.

Test: Level 2

An assistant hides up to five objects in a marked area that is no more than 30 square feet. You will not know how many objects you are looking for. You will bring the dog to the area and give him the command to fine-search; he will locate and alert on each object.

Police, military, and SAR dog handlers form a deep bond with their K9 partners. Each member of the team trusts the other with his or her life.

EVIDENCE SEARCH

efore starting evidence-search training, the dog must understand the concept that he is to find something that has human scent. Most dogs do not have difficulty finding objects with strong human scent on them. It will also help the dog if he knows how to fine search before being taught to evidence search.

There are two types of evidence searches. The first is when the dog is looking for an object connected to a crime scene. Typically, the object either is at the crime scene or has been discarded at another location.

The second type of evidence search is a missing-person situation. It is important to look for clues when searching for a missing person. Many handlers want their dogs to indicate anything that has human scent on it, such as a glove, hat, footprint, and so on. In a missing-person search, there is only one person to find, but many clues, and the clues provide critical information.

Regardless of the type of evidence search, the dog (and search team) must not touch or pick up any objects found. This means that the dog must not disturb the object by mouthing it, walking over it, or knocking it around. The location of the object could be important to the authorities, and the object may be sent to a laboratory for analysis.

In a missing-person search, the location of the article, if verified as belonging to the missing person, can shift the whole search effort in a new direction. In addition, if the article is not disturbed, a scent-specific dog can follow a scent trail from that point.

Level 1: Introducing the Article Search

Goal: To introduce article searching to the dog and fine-tune his small-area search skills.
Target Skill: The dog will learn the concept of finding an article.

Method

Either the assistant or you will tease the dog with an object that the dog finds interesting. Never use one of the dog's toys or something that he is allowed to pick up. When the dog is excited, the assistant tosses the object into moderate brush or grass that is high enough that the dog cannot see the object when it lands. However, the dog will see the object being tossed.

The minute the object hits the ground, give the dog either an article-search command or the missing-person command (wilderness airscenting). This is a matter of personal preference. If you want one command to mean both an article search

and a body search, then use the same command. If you want the dog to know when he is looking for a body versus an object, use a different command for each type of search.

As soon as the dog reaches the article, praise the dog. If you want the dog to do a refind for objects, wait until the dog finds objects readily, then hang back and let the dog come to you, give the alert, and lead you to the object. Because the dog already knows these steps, it is only a matter of showing him what to do and applying it.

At this level of training, teach the dog to leave the object where he finds it. If the dog has a difficult time not picking up the object, as can be the case with dogs who love to retrieve, work on the problem before proceeding with this level of training.

If the dog needs a new alert signal, show him what alert signal (previously taught) to use when he finds the object. After the dog knows the signal, you will apply it to the search. The dog will learn to stay by the article and not touch it while giving the signal.

Level 2: Hidden Articles

Goal: To solidify the dog's concept of finding objects.
Target Skill: The dog's search skills will be refined.

Method

Once the dog is proficient at Level 1, he is ready for this phase of training. Have an assistant place one to three objects, hidden from view, with some buried, in an area of about 30 square feet.

Take the dog to the area and give him the command for fine searching. The dog will know from previous training how to apply the fine-search technique to this situation.

Once the dog finds the article, he will give the alert, and you will praise or reward him. You will then release the dog from that article and continue to search until he finds all of the articles.

In another exercise, there will be no objects for the dog to find. It is not unusual on a mission to be asked to search an area that does not have anything in it. When the sector is completed, the dog will give the all-clear signal, if he has been taught to do it; otherwise, you must feel confident that the dog did not miss anything. After the exercise is finished, give the dog another short problem where he does find an object.

Test: Level 2

A problem is set up as just described, and you will not know where the objects are. Up to five objects will be on the ground, covered by leaves, hidden by grass, buried just below the surface, and otherwise concealed. You and your dog will find each object; the dog gives an alert for each. At no time will the dog touch the objects.

In another test, there will be no objects placed, and the dog will clear the area and give the all-clear signal. You will recognize and be confident that the dog did not miss any objects.

England's David Salisbury and SAR dogs. Working with teams from around the world is one of the pleasures of SAR work.

PART THREE

GOING
BEYOND

3

CHAPTER 18

ADDITIONAL COMMANDS FOR THE SAR DOG

Agility training is the basis for many of the additional commands. However, it is essential that the SAR dog handler realize that agility for working dogs is not the same as competitive agility for sport. Doing competitive agility with a SAR dog may be risky, as sport agility requires the dog to give a fast and showy performance. This is the opposite of SAR work, which requires that the dog move slowly and methodically and to think carefully about what he is doing. The purpose of training a SAR dog in agility exercises is to prepare the dog for disaster searching.

Rushing can cause injury or even death to the dog, the missing person, or the rescue personnel. Strong control and judgment on the part of the dog is required. The dog is trained to obey commands and be familiar with debris piles to the point at which he can make judgment calls about walking on surfaces. Keep in mind that if the

dog is working at a distance from you, he may see a danger that you cannot, such as a hole. When you and the dog have worked as a team long enough, the dog will learn intelligent disobedience.

The commands that follow are the major commands that a handler needs to teach to a SAR dog. Some of them are agility commands while others are additional commands unique to SAR work.

Back

Goal: To teach the dog to think about the placement of his hind feet and to back away from the object that he is looking at or the spot he is heading toward.
Target Skill: The dog will back up rather than turn around.

Method

Place two low, long objects, such as picnic benches, parallel with each other. The objects should be about shoulder height to the dog and as long as six or so of the dog's steps. The dog needs to be able to see over the objects. Be sure that the objects are not wobbly and cannot fall easily. If they are, have two assistants help hold them in place.

Place the objects far enough apart so that the dog can stand between them easily but cannot turn around. Then walk the dog on leash in between the objects until he goes through without hesitation. Do not let him jump over the objects.

When the dog is familiar and comfortable with the objects, place the dog between them with his nose even with the end of them so that the length of the objects is behind the dog. Stand directly in front of the dog and give him the *back* command while slowly walking forward, encouraging the dog to walk backward. Do not let the dog jump to the outside of the objects. As soon as the dog takes one step backwards, either praise him or click him (if clicker training).

After rewarding the dog, start the process over again, adding a step or two each time until the dog will back up for the entire length of the objects. Once the dog is backing up the whole way with one *back* command, remove the objects and again practice having him back up. Remember, moving slowly is the key to this exercise; the dog must have time to feel his hind feet and think about them.

Wait

Goal: To teach the dog to freeze in place for a few seconds.
Target Skill: The dog will freeze in position and wait for another command.

Method

This exercise is a variation of the *stay* or *stand for examination* exercise. The main difference is the position of the dog and the length of time for which the dog must hold the position.

On a *sit-stay*, the dog holds the sit position, while the *down-stay* command has the dog holding the prone or down position. With the *wait* command, the dog will stop in whatever position he is in, usually standing.

A tree or pole can help when teaching this exercise. Tie a long rope to the handle end of a leash and attach the leash to the dog's collar. Have the dog sit next to the tree (or pole) and loop the rope around the tree, forming a "U" shape. Have the dog sit far enough in front of the tree so that he will not be inclined to go back around the tree but will walk straight toward you.

Walk as far away from the dog as possible, holding enough rope so that the dog can reach you. Call the dog, and after the dog has taken a few steps, give the *wait* command while stopping the dog by holding the rope so that it cannot slide any farther around the tree.

As soon as the dog stops, praise or click the dog; then call the dog again and repeat the process until the dog reaches you, getting a huge reward.

When practicing this exercise, be sure not to give the *wait* command at the same distance from the dog each time. Vary this exercise as much as possible.

Once the dog understands the *wait* command, practice it without the rope in as many situations as possible.

Problems

The dog may run toward you so fast that you cannot say the *wait* command fast

Using a pulley and/or a tree, you can teach the dog to stop what he's doing and wait.

enough. If this happens, slow the dog down enough to get one *wait* command in before he reaches you. Do this by putting a putting a little bit of tension on the rope. However, be careful that the dog does not think that the tension is a jerk on the leash or a correction. If the dog continues to be too fast, using a longer rope will give the handler enough time to give the *wait* command.

Turn Around

Goal: To show the dog how to place his feet in a methodical manner and not to rush.

Target Skill: The dog will freeze in position and wait for another command.

Method

Before starting this exercise, teach the dog to walk on a board that is flat on the ground or raised only a few inches. Once the dog can walk on a 6-inch-wide board on the ground, place a 12-inch-wide board a few feet off the ground. The wider board is necessary for the beginning steps of teaching the dog to turn around; if you start out with too narrow a board, the dog might not want to turn around. The board should be at least twice as long as the dog. You can make the board stable by using cinder blocks or bricks to support it.

You and an assistant stand on either side of the dog. Give the dog a *wait* command if necessary to get the dog to stand quietly on the board. Next, give the dog the command to turn around and gently guide the his head around to lead him to turn around on the board. The goal is to get the dog to think about where he is placing his feet.

If the dog jumps off the board, start over. Ignore the dog if he jumps off, but encourage him for any attempt to turn around. If the dog consistently jumps off the board, switch to a board wide enough so that the dog will turn around. As the dog learns the command, progress to a narrower board.

Problems

Sometimes a dog will jump off the board at first. Because of a dog's speed and size, it is not a good idea to try to catch or stop the dog when the board is at a low level. Instead, put the board near or against a wall or something else that will stop the dog from jumping. Then, with the dog between you and the obstacle, gently guide the dog to turn around. As the dog progresses, raise the board and use an assistant to help in case the dog becomes frightened or jumps off the board.

Another method is to teach the dog the command to turn around on the ground before trying it on a board. Lure the dog in a tight half-circle with a treat. Once he will follow your hand with the treat, add the *turn around* command. When the dog has mastered this as well as possible on the ground, put him on a wide board and practice until he performs the command willingly. Then use boards of narrower widths until you're using as narrow a board as possible.

Go to an Object

Goal: To teach the dog to move away from the handler, either in a specific direction or by being redirected while away from the handler.

Target Skill: The dog will go to an object or location.

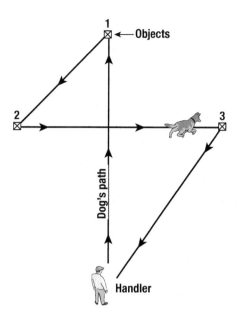

1 ◻ ◄—Objects

2 ◻—►

3 ◻

Dog's path

Handler

To teach the dog to go in a specific direction, the dog is sent to the center object (1), then sent to object 2 or 3, then sent to the opposite object, and finally recalled.

Method

Before attempting this exercise, decide which signals to use for changing direction. Some handlers have one signal for a right turn and another for a left turn. Some teach their dogs to go in the direction in which they are pointing. Keep in mind that if you have specific commands for *right* and *left* and your dog is facing you, the commands will be the opposite of what you want, as your right will be your dog's left and vice versa.

Some handlers use whistles, which work very well because a dog can hear a whistle no matter what kind of noise is present. Some people may be unsure about the effect that a whistle will have on other dogs, but whistles are successfully used on working dogs in tandem at sheepherding trials. Each dog knows his own whistle. In fact, an excellent type of whistle to use is a sheepdog whistle, found online through sheepherding suppliers.

This exercise is very easy to teach with clicker-training methods if the dog already understands clicker training. Once the dog has been clicker-trained to hit a target stick, then he is ready for this phase of training.

Place two sticks in the ground about 5 feet apart; each stick should have a Wiffle ball or an object of similiar size attached to its end. If the dog is well trained in clicker methods, he will go to the first stick and touch it (this is called *targeting* on a stick). When he does this, he gets a click. Then he will go to the next stick, touch it, and get a click.

If the dog is not trained to target on a stick, then either point to the stick or put a scent on it to attract the dog. Praise the dog as soon as he either goes to the stick or goes in the direction of the stick.

Once the dog does this reliably, add a command. When the dog goes to the stick on command, move the sticks apart but still within sight. Move back about 20 feet and send the dog to the first stick. When the dog reaches the stick, give the dog a *wait* command and then give him a command to go to the other stick.

As soon as the dog masters this level, remove the sticks and put flat objects in their place. Repeat the exercise. When the dog is going to the right or left object on command, vary the exercise by having the dog move from one object to another, giving a *wait* or *stay* command, getting him to stay by the object, and then having him return to you.

Add more objects to the problem as the dog masters the technique. The dog is required to be able to work with at least three objects. Work with this problem until the dog goes to an object, waits; goes to the next object, waits; and then goes back to a previous object and waits. The dog should be able to stop with a *wait* command on the way to an object as well.

Problems

Sometimes a dog will have difficulty understanding that he has to leave his handler. You can start by working with the sticks or objects close enough so that the dog will leave you. Once the dog gets the idea, it should not be a problem. If it is, use the *go* exercise.

Go

Goal: To teach the dog to leave the handler.
Target Skill: The dog will leave the handler to go to an object instead of to find a person.

Method

Stage this problem in an area that is clear of brush and high grass, such as on a hard surface. You can even do this exercise at home, indoors or on a patio.

With the dog sitting in the heel position, meaning that he is sitting by your side, toss a small piece of food as far in front of him as you can. If necessary, keep the dog on a leash with a quick-release snap. As soon as the food hits the ground, give the dog the *go* command and let him get the food. When the dog reaches the food, tell him to wait or stay. Then pause and call the dog. Once the dog associates the command with going away from you, make him wait before sending him to get the food.

After the dog has mastered the exercise with food, get a mat or some other low object that the dog can easily get onto and toss food onto the object, repeating the aforementioned steps. When the dog readily performs this exercise, start sending him to the object without using food.

Once the dog has mastered the *go* command, return to the *go to an object* exercise. Again, clicker training works very well with the *go to an object* command.

Look or Check

Goal: To teach the dog to look at a specific place or general location.
Target Skill: The dog will look at something specific, such as a footprint or a clump of brush.

Method

Either a clicker or food reward works well for this exercise. If using the clicker, place an interesting object on the floor or ground. When the dog investigates, he gets a click. The clicker-trained dog will notice this right away. Once the dog goes to the spot, either by looking at it or moving to it (depending on how far away the spot is), reliably, you can add the command.

If using food, put the dog on a *sit-stay* and place the food just out of reach on the floor in front of the dog, then point to the food and give the *look* command. The dog can eat the treat when he looks at it. Keep doing this until the dog will look without food present.

After the dog has mastered the *look/check* command, hide objects in grass or brush for the dog to find. The objects can be visible at first. Walk the dog to the area with the hidden objects and give him the *look* command while pointing to the area. When the dog finds an object and gives an alert (if trained to do so), reward him.

Handler Agnes with Seven, doing agility training in Holland.

Set up an exercise in which you have the dog look in some areas where objects are hidden and other areas where there are no objects hidden. The dog will give the trained alert based on the type of item found. The items that the handler can use are any items that the dog is trained to find, which could include evidence, cadaver, or any type of clue. If the dog is trained to give an all-clear signal, he will do so if there are no objects to find.

Slow

Goal: To teach the dog to move slowly.
Target Skill: The dog will respond to a command from the handler to slow down in certain situations.

Method

Begin in a *heel* type of exercise in which the dog is walking next to you and paying attention to you, as opposed to a "free" walk for entertainment. Do not let the dog slip into "obedience mode" if he has been given formal obedience training. Give him a command to slow down while you slow your pace. The dog needs to connect the action of slowing down with the command. Next, let the dog walk on a board and give the dog the *slow* command. Some handlers like to use the word *easy* for this. The word that you use is not important, but using the same word consistently is important.

same path of travel but to slow down.

Once the dog knows the *slow* command, practice it in different situations, teaching the dog to stop and then proceed slowly.

Climb a Ladder

Goal: To develop the dog's agility skills, teach him to place his feet, and develop his balance.
Target Skill: The dog will climb up and down a ladder.

Method

Obtain a ladder with flat wooden steps going both up and down. If you must use a ladder with metal steps, put non-skid pads on the steps until the dog is comfortable with the ladder, because many dogs do not like the feel of metal. Ideally, the ladder should be at a wide angle so that there's not such a sharp slope.

Start by letting the dog look at and sniff the ladder. If the dog is clicker-trained and he puts a paw on the ladder, he gets a click. If the dog is not clicker-trained, pat the rung of the ladder and lure the dog up. It is OK to use food as a lure. If the dog will not put his feet on the ladder on his own, gently place his front paws on one of the ladder rungs. As the dog feels comfortable with his feet on the rungs or steps, gently lead him up by putting slight pressure on his collar. If the dog panics, let him jump off the ladder, rest, and then try again. Sometimes a dog will just put his front paws on the first or

Dogs must learn to climb a ladder as part of their agility training for SAR. Handler Agnes with her German Shepherd Seven are at the international training exercise in Poland with the Polish Firebrigade and the German Technische Hilfswerke.

Next, set up the same type of barriers that you used in the *back* exercise so that the dog has to walk between them. As the dog walks between the objects, you can put your hand in front of him and give the *slow* command. Repeating this exercise will teach the dog to slow down on command. Placing the dog between barriers will help him focus on the command instead of moving in a different direction. The idea is to have the dog stay on the second step, and that is all you can do for a few training sessions until he feels safe doing that. With most dogs, as soon as they get both their front feet and hind feet on the ladder, they will usually progress quickly to climbing to the top. Once the dog climbs to the top, you can guide or hold him as he goes down the other side. It should only take a few tries for the dog to master this exercise.

Problems

If the dog seems frightened by the ladder, cut open large paper shopping bags (or other similar material) and tape them behind the steps so that the area between the steps looks closed. Often, smaller dogs will be afraid of the openness of the steps. Once the dog learns that he can walk up and down the ladder without falling through, you can remove the paper. Keep in mind that because a dog does not have good depth and distance perception, he could be unsure of what he sees. The openness between the rungs of the ladder can make the dog feel as though he will fall through.

If this technique does not work, have the dog climb ladderlike steps that lead to an elevated deck or have the ladder butt up against a platform that the dog can get onto when he reaches the top. Once the dog is comfortable with going up the ladder, add going down, either with the same ladder or a different one. When the dog can go up and down from the platform, have him go up and down the ladder without the platform.

Crawl Through

Goal: To build the dog's confidence in going into objects that do not have a visible exit.

Target Skill: The dog will go through tunnels that get increasingly narrower and incorporate turns.

Method

Some handlers like to teach their dogs a specific *crawl through* command so that they can tell their dogs from a distance to go through, rather than over or around, something. Use a culvert or another pipelike object that is wide enough for the dog to crawl through easily and is only 5 or 10 feet long. Place an assistant at the opposite end of the tunnel while you hold the dog. The assistant will call the dog to encourage him to go through the tunnel. If the dog is reluctant to leave you, the assistant will hold him while you call him.

You can use food or a toy to coax the dog through the tunnel, or you can put him on a long leash that goes through the tunnel so that you can gently pull on the leash while coaxing and encouraging the dog. Once the dog goes through, he gets a big reward.

When the dog is happily going through the tunnel, add turns and distance and make the tunnel narrower. When the dog masters these changes, put some debris in the tunnel so that he must work around it to get through the tunnel.

The next step will be to use a tunnel that is open at one end only. This means that the dog will have to enter the tunnel, turn around, and exit the same way he went in. This is often a situation that a dog will encounter in SAR work. After that, use an agility-type collapsible tunnel that is made of nylon or other fabric. This type of tunnel has a rigid opening, but the fabric is collapsed at the other end, requiring the dog to push through the fabric to get out.

Slick and Unstable Surfaces

Goal: To build the dog's confidence on slick and unstable surfaces.
Target Skill: The dog will learn that spreading his toes gives him control on slick and unstable surfaces.

Method

Place different materials, such as a plastic tarp, plywood, sheet metal, wire mesh, or any other material unfamiliar to the dog, on the ground. Lead the dog over these surfaces, encouraging him to walk on them. Once the dog will do this willingly, cover some of the surfaces with aluminum foil and have him walk over them again. This will create unfamiliar noise for the dog to become accustomed to.

Next, enlarge these surfaces and put them on a slant. As the dog feels himself start to slide, he will naturally spread his toes to gain control. The dog must prac-

tice as much as necessary so that he will not hesitate to do this exercise or to walk on unfamiliar surfaces during actual missions.

Moving Surfaces

Walking a Board

Goal: To reinforce for the dog that he is not to jump off narrow objects and that he is to slow down when the board bounces.
Target Skill: The dog will walk on a bouncing board that is 8 inches wide or less (depending upon the size of the dog).

Method

Be sure that the dog is comfortable and willing to walk on a stable board before doing this exercise. Start with a board that is wide enough for the dog to feel safe. The width will depend on the size of the dog. Be sure to secure the board and have the dog walk back and forth on it. As the dog does this willingly, remove some of the supports in the middle of the board so that it will bounce a little. (Always be sure that the board is secure so that the ends will not fall.) When the dog is comfortable walking on a bouncing board, practice the *wait, turn around, slow,* and *back* commands.

Once the dog has mastered this level, remove more supports from the board so that the bouncing increases. Once the board starts to bounce, give the dog the *slow* command. The dog will associate instability with slowing down.

Dave Salisbury and Flick, training with the German Red Cross unit at Dresden. Note the required height for the agility test equipment.

As soon as the dog masters the bouncing board, go back to the wide, stable board and put objects of various heights on it. Have the dog walk the board, stepping over the objects. This will teach the dog to walk along a narrow surface littered with debris. If the dog is very secure doing this exercise, you can use boards that are narrower in width, again gauged by the size of the dog.

Teeter-Totter 1

Goal: To teach the dog to pause and balance on a moving surface.
Target Skill: The dog will walk a teeter-totter and wait in the middle to practice keeping his balance.

Method

Have the dog master the bouncing board exercise before progressing to the teeter-totter. The handler can use a common teeter-totter such as that found on a playground, use an agility teeter-totter, or make a teeter-totter that is similar to either type. Lead the dog to one end of the teeter-totter and guide him onto the board. Giving the dog the *slow* command, have him walk onto the teeter-totter. Once the dog reaches the middle, have him wait so that he can to keep the board level by shifting his weight. Most dogs will do this automatically. After he's waited a few seconds in the middle, have the dog walk to the other end and off the teeter-totter.

The dog will be nervous at first, so only do this exercise a few times in a training session. Do not go on to the teeter-totter 2 exercise until the dog masters this level.

Teeter-Totter 2

> **Goal:** To increase the dog's ability to balance and experience complex movement.
> **Target Skill:** The dog will become familiar with a teeter-totter that moves in two directions.

Method

Place the teeter-totter board on a small barrel or similar object in such a way that the barrel causes the board to move back and forth as it also moves up and down. Have the dog walk the board while the barrel moves back and forth. If necessary, assistants can move the barrel a little with ropes or a stick. The dog must be able to walk, slow down, wait, and turn around on the moving teeter-totter.

Take It

> **Goal:** To prepare the dog for the *hold it* exercise.
> **Target Skill:** The dog will put an object into his mouth on command.

Method

Tease the dog with an object; in this case, it can be a toy. Just as the dog is about to take the object, give him the *take* it command. After a few tries, the dog should take an object offered to him. Once he does this, place the object on the ground and tell him to take it. If the dog is unsure, wiggle the object to get his attention. If necessary, point to the object and encourage the dog to take it. Remember to praise and reward the dog each time he takes the object.

Hold It

> **Goal:** To provide an exercise to help teach the dog to carry objects as part of an alert signal.
> **Target Skill:** The dog to hold an object in his mouth on command.

Method

Once a dog is willing to take an object in his mouth, you can teach him to hold it by gently placing your hand under the dog's chin while giving him a *hold it* command. Be sure not to force the dog's mouth shut or hurt the dog in any way. If the dog holds the object loosely, wiggle it, and the dog will most likely clamp down. Immediately praise or click the dog and then let him release the object.

Gradually have the dog hold the object for longer periods until he will walk with the object in his mouth.

Out

> **Goal:** To teach a dog to release an object that is in his mouth.
> **Target Skill:** The dog will drop on command anything that he has taken.

Method

Start this exercise with food. If a dog will give up food, he will give up anything else. Use food with substance, such as a dog biscuit or hard cheese. Have the dog in a sit-stay position in front of you. Place a tiny bit of the food between your thumb and index finger, sandwiching the food with your fingers on the top and bottom.

Offer the food to the dog without opening your fingers. The dog will put his mouth over your fingers and as soon as he feels the fingers, he will open his mouth. The instant that the dog opens his mouth, give the *out* command and immediately give the dog the food. This way, the dog learns that if he gives up the food, he will get the treat.

As the dog gets the idea and readily gives up the food, let a small bit of the food extend from between your fingers, but only enough so that the dog's front teeth can feel the food. The second the dog puts his teeth on the food, give the *out* command and then give the dog the food (or a small piece of better food) when he backs off.

Continue this exercise until the dog will drop food that is in his mouth. Then use non-food items and have the dog take, hold, and release the various items.

For some dogs, this exercise is easily accomplished with a ball. Toss the ball for the dog to retrieve. When he comes back, wait for him to drop the ball or take it from him. Throw the ball again until the dog learns that by giving up the ball,

the game will continue. When the dog drops the ball, add the *out* command. If you can time the *out* command to the second before the dog drops the ball, it will work better. Be sure that, each time the dog "outs," or gives up, an object, he gets a reward that is better than what he gave up.

Fetch

Goal: To combine the *go, take it, hold it, come,* and *out* commands.

Target Skill: The dog will retrieve an article.

Method

Some dogs fetch naturally, while others want nothing to do with fetching things. If the dog is a natural retriever, he may be able to be taught to fetch before he's taught the *out* command.

Tease the dog with an object that he likes. As soon as the dog is interested in the object, toss it a short distance away. Give the dog the *go* command if necessary, and when the dog reaches the object, tell him to take it, then tell him to hold it, and then call him back. When the dog returns, give him the *out* command and praise him.

In most cases, the dog will do all of this naturally, and you will need only to introduce the word *fetch* for the dog to make the association that the *fetch* command tells him to perform this sequence of actions.

Jump

Method

Set up low jumps, no higher than the dog's elbow, at different distances apart but never so close together that the dog does not have room to land and take off. Lead the dog to the first jump and encourage him to jump over it, giving him a *jump* command. Continue to the rest of the jumps. Once the dog can handle jumps at this height, increase the height to his shoulder.

If the dog seems confused about what he is to do, you can walk over the jumps with the dog on leash. Alternatively, if it is not easy for you to do this, you can stand on the other side of a jump and call the dog over, with the dog on leash.

Once the dog knows the *jump* command and readily jumps obstacles, you can design exercises that use the *wait* and *recall* commands, as well as the directional commands, to keep the dog's interest.

Speak

Method

There are a number of ways to teach a dog to speak on command. The easiest is to use the clicker. Create a noise that will get the dog to bark, and click when he barks. It will only take a few tries for the dog to get the idea. Once the dog offers a bark, either on his own or in response to a prompt/tease from you, you can add the *speak* command.

If the dog is not clicker-trained, you can tease him with a very desirable treat. When the dog gets frustrated enough, he will bark. As soon as the dog barks, praise him and give him the treat. Once the dog barks reliably, either by prompt or tease, add the *speak* command. It should only take the dog several repetitions to make the connection between the command and the action of barking.

Quiet

Method

Once the dog will speak on command, you can teach him to be quiet on command, as well. Give the dog the *speak* command and then, while he is barking, take a treat and put it near his nose. It is not possible for a dog to sniff and bark at the same time. As soon as the dog stops barking, give him the treat. Add the *quiet* command just as he is about to stop barking.

Leave It

Goal: To give the handler a way to proof the dog against objects that are not to be touched and to build the dog's self-control.

Target Skill: The dog will ignore an object on command.

Method

This lesson is easiest to do using a head harness on the dog. If he is not used to this training device, introduce it to him and have him wear it while performing obedience exercises so that he's comfortable with it. The head harness will allow you to redirect the dog's gaze away from the forbidden object, thus teaching him to turn away from it. Allowing the dog to watch the object as he is taken away from it may hinder him from making the connection that he is to turn away from it quickly. This is because when you pull the dog back on a buckle collar, he is still focused on and thinking of the object. Being pulled away is only a nuisance to him.

Place an object that is new and interesting to the dog at a distance from the training area. It can be outside or indoors. With the dog in a heel position, walk toward the object, but do not acknowledge the object. The dog should not think that you purposely walked to the object.

The instant the dog notices or shows interest, even mild interest, in the object, sternly tell him to leave it (or give another similar command) and immediately back up very quickly. The idea is to communicate urgency to the dog, as if the two of you came upon a poisonous snake. As soon as the dog turns away and does not try to look at the object, stop and praise the dog lavishly.

Do this exercise with as many objects that will interest the dog as you can find. Never allow the dog to have or even make contact with the objects. The message is "get away from it now!"

As soon as the dog has mastered the *leave it* command, make the objects even more tempting. An assistant is necessary at this point. Take a piece of fake fur or real fur from an old coat collar, tie it into a bundle, and then tie a small string to the bundle. Have an assistant hide out of sight, downwind from the dog (breeze blowing from the dog to the assistant). As soon as the dog notices the object, or at the beginning of the walk, the assistant will pull the fur, creating a jerking motion. The instant the dog looks at the object, give the *leave it* command and walk in the opposite direction. At the same time that you give the *leave it* command, the assistant will stop making the fur move. As soon as the dog ignores the fur on command, the assistant will keep moving the fur. The idea is to simulate having the dog come across a small animal in the field. This will also allow the dog to build his self-control. Remember, obedience is not a matter of having the dog understand a command, but the dog's ability to exercise self-control between what he wants to do and what you want him to do.

CHAPTER 19

GAME CHASING AND BURNOUT

ometimes it is difficult for a dog to control his urge to chase small or even large animals. Many breeds of dog have been bred to hunt and/or find and kill small animals. Terriers, for example, are used to kill rodents that live in and near farms. Because of this inbred trait, some dogs cannot resist the urge to chase game or other forms of wildlife. This is not acceptable for SAR dogs, and if the problem is caught early, it can be corrected.

Scientists have learned that dogs are much more intelligent than we ever imagined. With a higher level of intelligence can come other types of problems. One problem that can plague a SAR dog is burnout. Just like humans, dogs can suffer from being overworked. This chapter will discuss both game chasing and burnout.

Game Chasing

A dog that chases game is not reliable as a search dog. Game chasing is not a problem seen only in wilderness searching; it can be a problem for disaster dogs, as well. Often, rodents live in disaster sites.

Unfortunately, a game-chasing habit can develop at any time in a dog's life. However, a well-trained dog that is proofed against game chasing is less likely to start doing it than one who is not proofed against it.

Never forget that game chasing is a result of a dog's natural prey drive. Most handlers select dogs with high prey drives because they feel that this is a requirement for a good search dog. Resisting the urge to chase game requires a keen balancing act on the part of the dog between instinct to chase prey and self-control.

Building a strong drive to find humans early in the dog's SAR training, and keeping this drive high, will help the dog ignore the urge to chase other animals. Teaching a dog not to chase game will not prevent the dog from alerting you to the presence of danger from a predator if you live in an area in which this is a problem.

Prevention is the best method. Make certain that no family member or friend makes a game of letting the dog chase squirrels or other animals. Also, before the dog is obedience-trained, never let him off leash in an environment where he can encounter wild animals. It does not take much experience for a dog to learn that he likes chasing game. After all, it strikes a deep chord in the heart of a dog with a high prey drive.

Do not allow the dog to roam freely around farm animals when he is young. As soon as the dog is controllable, introduce him to livestock and other wild animals that are accessible to you, but never allow him the freedom to chase them. If the dog shows any interest in chasing the animals, give the *leave it* command. Remember to always praise the dog for looking away from the animal or for coming to you when called away from an animal.

If you live in an area where you have many squirrels, be careful that some daring squirrels are not teasing the dog through windows or doors. This can frustrate even the best dog, causing him to be a squirrel-hater for life. Never encourage the dog to chase any common animals, whether squirrels or other critters found in your area.

Introduce the dog at the earliest age possible to all types of small animals in a way that he will consider them companions rather than prey. The idea is to build the dog's tolerance for them as well as his self-control.

In the past, handlers have used various methods to try to break a dog from the habit chasing game or small animals. The following methods are not recommended:

1. A veterinarian injects the dog with a substance that makes him very sick

Changing up training areas and finding new hiding spots can renew a dog's enthusiasm for his work.

just before he is allowed to chase game. The theory is that the dog will get so sick that he will associate the illness with chasing game or the scent of the game and, as a result, will never want to chase game again. The success of this method depends upon the dog's independently making the connection between the game and the illness. It rarely works.

2. Shock the dog with an electronic shock collar to deter the dog from chasing game.

3. Take the dead animal and tie it to the dog's neck, letting it hang for a few days.

There are trainers who swear by these methods. However, even if done by an expert, these methods can and do cause severe mental damage to a dog and are not reliable.

To teach a dog not to chase game, teach the *leave it* command. When the dog masters the command at the "moving fur" level, you can use live animals in a safe cage to proof the dog. Another method is to walk the dog on leash in an area where game is plentiful. Tame squirrels that live in parks and are familiar with dogs and people work well.

Once the dog can handle small animals in cages or close by, introduce him to large animals, even if only from a distance. As soon as the dog looks at the animals, give the *leave it* command. Practice simple obedience exercises in the presence of all types of animals, including ones that are quiet as well as ones that are moving.

If the dog cannot ignore animals, train him at a distance from the animals such that the dog barely notices them. Once the dog can handle this, incrementally work closer to the animals until he can control himself next to them.

If the dog will not give up chasing animals and is not reliable off leash around animals, do not use the dog for SAR work. A handler who spends the bulk of the mission following deer trails is a detriment rather than an asset to the mission; such behavior can put the missing person's life at risk.

Burnout

If a dog has been reliable and working well, and then he suddenly stops working or loses his "edge," it is time to reassess the dog and/or the situation. The first step is to review Chapter 4 to see if it is a handling error on your part. At the same time, have the dog examined by a veterinarian to be sure that he is not suffering from a physical ailment. If these things are fine, then it is time to look at the training exercises.

Sometimes a dog will become familiar with a training area and all of the hiding places and thus become bored with his training. This can be a problem for units that do not have access to many large training sites and must use the same area frequently. The dog also could be bored with the exercises because they are too routine and predictable. He always finds the same people and does not get new, "strange" people to find.

Although it is rare, a seasoned search dog may not take training exercises seriously. Some dogs are very perceptive and know the difference between training and real missions. Training sessions do not have the excitement that actual missions do.

Another possibility is that the dog needs a vacation. This can happen when a dog trains a few times a week and more earnestly on the weekends. Dogs do not forget what they've learned, so a vacation will not necessitate retraining the dog.

If the dog does not resume his earlier enthusiasm for SAR work and becomes unreliable, it may be time to retire him. Age is not always a factor in making this decision, but a dog's performance is always an indicator of whether or not he should be used in the field. Dogs are not machines, and a dog's change of heart toward the work could result from a combination of issues, some of which you may never know about.

Although Ness was the grandson of a famous sheepherding dog (Gilchrist's Spot), Larry was able to teach him to completely ignore the livestock and wild animals they encountered on missions.

CHAPTER 20

MANAGEMENT OF THE SEARCH MISSION

here are courses and textbooks available about how to manage a search operation. This chapter will highlight this aspect of search and rescue to give you an idea of what should take place. The information provided in no way replaces the official training needed to be an incident commander (IC) or search manager; rather, it is a guide to what a potential SAR handler needs to know about search missions.

If you do not understand the concepts, methods, and terminology in this chapter, then you are not qualified to manage a search! Even if you don't want to manage a search, a course in management is necessary. A course will teach you how the Incident Command System (ICS) and a mission function. That way, you will have a better understanding about the kind of information to report to the command post and how to be an asset instead of a liability.

Larry Bulanda and Harlan Hemple analyze data on a search mission.

It is essential for productive teamwork that everyone in the search unit understand the whys and hows of running a mission. A rescue person must always be ready for the callout. A prompt response can mean the difference between life and death for the missing person. To make it easier, some people keep their gear in portable plastic boxes and their clothing handy. This way, when the call comes, they can get ready quickly and go. The box must contain all of the essentials so that the handler is ready for any type of mission, weather, and geographic location. Some handlers keep extra clothing in their boxes according to the season, while others take everything with them all of the time.

Members are required to know the standard operating procedures (SOPs) for their unit by heart. When members arrive at the meeting place, their training will have prepared them to know what to do, and then the unit will proceed to the search site. If the members are going to arrive at the search site individually, which is sometimes necessary, there is a procedure for setting up base or reporting to a specific individual.

Not every unit has someone who is qualified to act as IC or search manager. The unit must be honest about this and only offer management support if they can fulfill it. Keep in mind that the IC has both moral and legal responsibility. Even if the unit does not have a qualified IC, a preplan must be in place to aid the unit on a search mission. The preplan will be a study of the area that the unit serves; this is a written document (updated on a regular basis) that includes the following:

1. Search history for the area, listing the different types of searches (for example, drowning, wilderness, and suicide).
2. Special geographic features, such as caves, mines, gullies, and water.
3. The type of people who live in the area and other demographics (are there seasonal people, elderly people, outdoor attractions?).
4. Possible types of searches. Not every unit will respond to every type of search. Some units search in mountains, some units search in the desert, and some areas may rarely, if ever, have water searches. By surveying the types of missions in the area covered, SAR members will know what type of training and equipment they need.
5. Available resources. Units will retire old equipment, perhaps stop using certain equipment, and purchase new equipment. It is always good to know which units have what equipment. It also helps to know what response time another unit has.

KEEP IT QUIET

You must never talk to the media or the missing person's family members. There are two designated staging areas—one for family members and one for the media—and one specific SAR person will be assigned to each staging area. Often the media will hound the search personnel to find out details about the mission. In every case, at every level of the mission, the information that is exchanged between searchers is confidential. Until the missing person is found, SAR personnel have no way of knowing what actually took place, and what started as a SAR mission could wind up as a police incident. If information is leaked to the media, the family might become very upset. Often the media does not report the facts accurately and could hinder the search effort and/or upset the family needlessly.

Never allow family members to assist in the search mission or deploy in the field. This is for trained personnel only. Even if a family member is qualified to search, do not let him participate in the search. Family members are too emotionally involved to make objective decisions. Also, SAR personnel cannot discuss the case frankly if a family member is present. SAR personnel must be professional at all times and make important decisions about what they do and do not do.

All members of a unit will know how to meet and organize at a search when another unit is managing the mission. There is only one person who is authorized to contact the IC or command post when at a base camp. It is unprofessional for all of the members of a unit to flood the IC.

There is one IC for each mission. If it is a very large operation, then each unit will have a search manager who reports to the IC. Without the leaders (IC, search managers, and so on), there would be confusion, wasted time, and wasted resources.

It is the IC's responsibility to:

• Run the search mission, which means staying at base
• Oversee the efforts of the team(s)
• Plan a strategy based on input from the various logistics teams
• Use the resources available to find the missing person
• Do the best job possible
• Have a preplan to use on a SAR mission
• Realize that one person cannot accomplish a mission
• Be highly experienced in SAR and skilled at working with all types of people
• Keep a cool head and evaluate the situation in order to make the proper decisions
• Put together the search overhead team
• Know where to get qualified people when needed

The overhead team typically consists of at least the following:

• IC—the boss
• Plans team—responsible for developing the search plan
• Operations person—oversees the execution of the plans
• Logistics person—responsible for getting equipment and recourses
• Investigation person or team—gathers information about the missing person
• Communications expert—handles all modes of communications
• Media contact person—the only one who handles outside inquiries
• Safety—a person or team who makes sure that all SAR personnel who deploy have the correct equipment, are physically fit (including the dog), and are field-ready. In certain situations, the safety person/ team will assess the search situation. An example of this would be a collapsed structure expert who determines if it is safe to enter a building or part of a building at a disaster site
• Technical specialist—reviews technical issues such as specialized search equipment or situations

SAR personnel understand that the faster that teams deploy, the greater the chance there is that the missing person will be found. The longer the missing person is lost, and if the person is moving, the search area becomes exponentially larger if the team does not know in which

The Phoenixville Fire Department K-9 SAR Unit's overhead team, planning search strategies.

direction the missing person is traveling. While it is important to get teams into the field as quickly as possible, it is equally important not to make hasty decisions.

On the initial callout, the IC will obtain as much information about the missing person as possible. A lost-person questionnaire is very helpful; this can be purchased from SAR suppliers.

The first thing that an IC must do at the search site is establish a base area. This must be located near the site of the incident, but away from it. By keeping all activity away from the point last seen (PLS) or last known position (LKP), people will not inadvertently destroy clues that might exist on site.

The only activity at the site is connected to the job at hand—finding the missing person.

The following is a suggested order in which a search should proceed:

1. Base is set up and manned.
2. A command post is established. This is where the overhead team and search leaders meet. No one else goes into the command post.
3. A staging area is set up for everyone else. Searchers do not wander around the area.
4. Hasty teams are deployed, confinement is established, and the investigation is started.
5. A person is assigned to keep a record of all personnel on site. The log contains:
   - When personnel arrive on the search site
   - What time they are deployed to search and where

- What time they return from searching and their results
- When personnel leave the search site

6. A person is assigned to keep track of resources, including what resources are on site, what is en route, and when resources are available.

7. The overhead team determines the action to take based on the missing person's profile, the geographic features of the area, the weather, lost-person behavior, the date the person went missing, and so on.

8. The missing-person profile is updated, based on current information and information learned by the investigation team.

9. Several factors are determined, such as the maximum time needed to find the missing person alive, how large the search area is, and what the probability of detection (POD) is.

10. The boundaries of the search area are staffed for confinement.

11. The search area is segmented for SAR personnel to search.

12. The probability of area (POA), which will identify the areas to search first, is determined.

13. The phases of the mission—in other words, initial response, hasty search, and continual operational periods— are planned. An operational period is usually twelve hours. After the SAR personnel have worked for twelve hours, the next team, who is on standby, relieves them. This includes the overhead team and the IC. Often this is the most difficult thing to do on a mission. People are reluctant to let go and go home.

Some missions will run continuously, twenty-four hours a day, for a number of days. It is up to the incident commander and other officials involved in the mission (this could be politicians, law-enforcement officials, and so on) to decide how long a mission will run before it is called off. It is very difficult to call off a mission when the person is still missing. Often the reason why a mission is called off is that, based on the data collected throughout the mission, it is determined that the person is no longer in the area, or because resources have been exhausted.

At some point, the focus of the mission may change from a rescue to a recovery; this will downgrade the urgency. It could become a criminal situation, in which case the use of SAR teams may not be needed, and it becomes strictly a police matter. In this case, a SAR team could be called back to assist in searching for evidence or a cadaver.

It is essential that someone or a team of people document the entire search mission. They will keep a log (such as is outlined in item 5 in the list). Each operating team will document their part of the mission and turn the documents in to the command post. For example, the logistics person will record the name and contact information of the other units

MOUNTED UNITS

One of the tools for SAR is the use of mounted units. These people are horse lovers, and they use their horses for search missions. While a horse cannot search an area the same way that a dog can, horses do offer a few advantages. For one, the rider has a higher point of view and can often see further than the dog handler can.

Two mounted riders can act as the anchor points for a grid team. They are easy to see, which helps to keep the line straight and in the grid pattern. In less open areas, a mounted team can do a hasty search on trails, often more quickly than foot searchers can. Although horses do not give alerts the same way a dog does, they can, by their body language, alert their riders that something is in the area.

Not every horse is suitable for SAR missions. A potential SAR horse must be calm in spite of the activity of the search area, especially at base. The horse must be comfortable around dogs and people. The horse must be steady and not flighty or easily spooked. He must also be sure-footed; able to cross water, such as streams, creeks, and small rivers; and physically fit.

If SAR dog handlers live in an area where there are mounted units, it is a good idea for everyone to train together so that both the dogs and the horses learn to be comfortable around each other.

that responded to the mission and their time of arrival and departure. It is important to keep an account of everyone who goes into the field and when they return so that no one is left in the field, possibly injured. It is common for radio contact to be interrupted, so careful records must be written down to keep track of where everyone is located. The search plans, as well as all changes to the search plans, are recorded, and maps marked to show search sectors. The location(s) of all clues is recorded, and this data is reanalyzed constantly.

A search mission is an evolving event that can change with new information. In the event that the mission is suspended (hopefully because the missing person was found), the IC or search manager must stay at the site until all personnel are accounted for. This includes any units or personnel that may be on the way to the mission.

CHAPTER 21

POLITICS AND REWARDS

O ver the years, a number of people have asked me to add a section about the politics of search and rescue to this book. This is a difficult and touchy subject, but nonetheless, it exists. It has been my experience that the politics of SAR are the same worldwide. I suspect that this is true because human nature is the same worldwide!

For the most part, the politics of SAR are broken down into two types: the type that occurs between separate units that respond to a mission and the type that occurs within a unit.

Politics between Units

Particular agencies may prefer to work with particular units. This could be for a number of reasons, such as they work well together, they train together, or they are geographically near to each other and usually are called out together. When the situation arises where units that do not know each other must work together,

sometimes the members of each unit will be a little withdrawn and unsure of each other. This is especially true if they are unsure of each other's capabilities. Certifications and training are fine, but they do not always mean that a person is capable in the field.

Often, on a mission, the IC does not want to give up command to another person or another unit. The mission becomes his "baby." The IC may not have faith in the incoming IC or is so emotionally involved that he cannot let go. He may fear that the next person will not make the "right" decisions or will mess up all of his good work. This feeling is not limited to the IC; it will travel down the chain of command.

In some areas of the country, the advent of urbanization, cell phones, and GPS receivers, as well as a simple lack of places to get lost, has caused the number of search missions to drastically decrease, while the number of people who want to participate in SAR has increased. This has led many people to start their own units, often with multiple units being formed in the same area. Mission-stealing is the result. Each unit will try to persuade the local agencies (fire departments, police departments, park rangers, and so on) that they are the best and most available. It often becomes a matter of who has the best campaign or who has the best human-relations or sales skills. However, it is not unusual that the unit with the best advertising is the worst or least qualified in the field.

The sad thing is that these units will not train together and, for fear of losing territory, will not call each other on missions, even if needed. One of the major reasons why this happens, besides the fear of losing territory, is that a qualified unit is afraid to call out a unit whose search tactics or skills are inferior or unprofessional, thus giving their own unit a bad name.

There is also the problem of one unit, usually the inferior unit, trying to pirate members from the more advanced unit. Another situation that happens is that someone will join a unit with a good reputation, learn all he can, become qualified, and then start a competing unit.

These situations exist with all types of rescue units and are not limited to canine SAR units. However, because canine units are not regulated, they probably have more unqualified people in them than other types of units, such as fire departments, dive squads, or ambulance squads, which require state certifications and training. However, this is changing, as organizations such as the National Search Dog Alliance provide training, testing, and certification.

Unqualified units also come about because a handler trainee feels that his dog is mission-ready or is more advanced than the unit trainer believes or than the team's test results show. Often the excuse for a failed test is that the dog is having a bad day or something along those lines. Such a trainee will form his own unit, naming himself as head trainer or

Dave Salisbury (LEFT) and Michael Moore (RIGHT) at a joint training with German and Polish teams.

founder even though he does not have the skills, experience, or qualifications to do so. This is why it is important to check the documented and truthful qualifications of any unit or "trainer." Ask how long he has been involved in SAR work, what certifications he has, and how long he has been a SAR dog trainer and/or handler in a specific discipline.

Be sure to ask why this person is not part of an established unit. How does he receive callouts? No ethical unit ever deploys itself on a search. The unit is always requested by a specific agency, such as the police or fire department. Self-deployment not only is unethical but also is dangerous to everyone involved in the search mission. A unit that self-deploys shows that its members lack the proper training and credibility. Such a unit also gives volunteer search units a bad name, making it difficult for everyone.

Politics within the Unit

Every type of rescue unit has those people who only show up for actual missions and do not participate in training, the maintenance of equipment, or any of the other chores necessary to keep the unit functioning. They do the least amount of work required to remain qualified. These people are not team players. Some people only show up for major missions and then want to be either in the spotlight or assigned to the choice areas with the highest POD. These people are often referred to as "headline hoggers." Some of these types will show up at a mission and make sure that they are in view of the media, yet they never deploy on the search. These people will even go so far as to make outlandish claims about their "finds." Serious units must have a way to weed these people out, as they are liabilities and create bad feelings among the unit members. They also give canine SAR a bad name.

Sometimes a searcher will become qualified to search in a recognized unit and then show up on a local mission and try to pass himself off as an IC because of his affiliation when he does not have the qualifications. This does not happen often, but it does happen.

When it comes to dogs, the politics take on another dimension. Often, a dog handler will try to make it look as though his dog is the hero because the dog is his alter ego. Some people claim that only one breed of dog can do the work and will only consider calling other units who use all breeds as a last resort. Even though these people have a breed-specific attitude about SAR work, many of these same people would fight breed-specific legislation if their breed was the target.

Often, with agencies and within the unit, the politics revolve around personal likes and dislikes. Of course, it's human nature that we all have likes and dislikes, but when likes and dislikes are coupled with dominant, type-A personalities (which are attracted to SAR), the result can be a charged atmosphere. However, these types of people are the ones who will get out there and get the job done.

Sometimes a unit can become affected by power plays. One of the things that triggers this is when one member of the unit begins doing additional training outside of the unit. He will attend seminars, use available study resources, and even train with another unit. When he tries to share

Susan Bulanda with the SAR team from Poland at an international SAR competition in England at which she was a judge.

the information that he's learned, other unit members may feel threatened instead of being glad that a member is trying to do a better job. A solid unit will let this member teach the other members what he's learned so that everyone grows together.

Professional rescue people must work together and must put the missing person first, putting aside all personal feelings. They must view the find as a team find, and their effort as a team effort, because with a professional, quality unit, it *is* a team effort.

With all of this in mind, every search manager or IC can be faced with difficult situations. Sometimes more than one agency will call units to respond to a search without coordinating their efforts. If the IC or search manager finds out that unqualified teams or people have responded, he will have to decide how to handle the situation. The IC's ethics demand that he does not allow unqualified people to participate in a search mission. The wise IC or search manager will have a plan in place so that he can handle such situations in a way that will not cause problems and will maintain the safety of the mission.

The Rewards of SAR

Over the years, we have spoken with many people who are involved or have been involved in search and rescue work, both with and without dogs. While everyone has personal reasons for getting involved, there seems to be a few common threads among most of the people who participate in SAR.

Some do it because they enjoy helping other people. They enjoy using their skills or hobby to do a "real" job. For example, a diver may want to take his sport a step further, a veteran medic may want to share his skills and abilities with the community, a communications expert may want to handle the radio, or a canine handler wants to do real work instead of sport work with his dog. All agree that the rewards are worth the personal expense, time, and effort it takes to become a part of a professional volunteer organization. In some cases, a rescue person is employed by a rescue squad or fire department; for those people, this is the ultimate situation— being paid to do a job he loves.

The bond between Elane Flower and Sizzle is obvious.

People enjoy search work because it is a real-life ultimate mystery. They rise to the urgency and excitement of a search mission. They enjoy the adrenaline rush that comes with a callout. They relish the sense of belonging and unity among rescue personnel regardless of their differences. They thrive on search work because of the teamwork of the unit and because they love being outdoors. Some people also enjoy the element of danger that is involved.

There is a lighter side to SAR work, as well. Often the canine handler is asked to give talks and demonstrations. On one such occasion, I gave a talk to a group of young adults who were attending a State Trooper-sponsored camp. After the talk, a student laid a scent path and my SAR dog followed it to find the youth.

When that demonstration was finished, a trooper had an unusual request. It

Dave Hancock and Gus, working pals from Durham Search and Rescue and North Carolina SAR Dog Association.

seemed that all of the youngsters were responsible for putting their clothes away, but one boy had left a pair of shorts in the shower. No one would come forward to claim them, so the trooper asked if the dog could identify the owner of the underwear from a lineup.

Much to the amusement of the girls, the boys lined up in two rows. On the way to the beginning of the line of boys, the dog let me know that the boy's scent was in one particular cabin; it turned out that the "guilty" boy slept in that cabin.

The dog was scented on the shorts and proceeded to walk down the line of boys. I did all I could do to keep a straight face as we passed each boy. There were many sighs of "whew" and "oh boy" as the dog passed by.

As the dog started down the next line, he stopped in front of the guilty party. The dog was correct. The whooping and laughter was quite something as the guilty party was "apprehended." Later, the trooper told me that as soon as the boy knew the dog was going to be used, he confessed—dogs usually have that effect on the guilty! As far as the dog goes, it seemed as though he had a gleam of mischief in his eyes.

The bond that develops between dog and handler is like nothing else. The dog can go through a metamorphosis in behavior and attitude from the silly companion to the serious working dog. All working dogs are a beauty to behold as they do their jobs; their passion and love for the work is obvious to everyone.

ABOVE: England's David Salisbury and SAR dog Flick, resting after training. BELOW: Many SAR dogs double as therapy dogs and are especially good with children. Most youngsters enjoy hugging a furry friend.

APPENDIX A:
TRAINING OUTLINE

The following are suggested outlines for various types of SAR dog training. Airscent training provides a solid foundation and a good place to start for all types of SAR work, as this is where the dog learns the concept that he must find a human.

Airscenting Dogs–Wilderness

1. Start obedience training
2. Beginner runaway
3. Novice runaway
4. Teach the mechanics of the alert (*Can be done any time before it is needed in the training scenario.*)
5. Intermediate runaway
6. Advanced runaway
7. Beginning refind
8. Refind indication
9. Advanced refind
10. Trail problem
11. Beginning area problem
12. Advanced area problem
13. Beginning night problem
14. Advanced night problem
15. Heavy brush problem
16. Multiple missing persons problem
17. Beginning moving assistant
18. Intermediate moving assistant
19. Advanced moving assistant
20. More advanced moving assistant

Scent-Discrimination Dog–Wilderness

1. Start obedience training
2. Runaway
3. Scent article runaway
4. Teach the mechanics of the alert (*Can be taught any time before it is needed in the training scenario.*)
5. Identification
6. Tougher trail problem
7. No scent article
8. Aged scent path
9. More complicated scent path
10. Contaminated scent path
11. Unknown person
12. Identification from a group
13. Contaminated scent article
14. Tougher contaminated scent article

Water Search Training

1. Qualify in wilderness training
2. Preparation for water training
3. Beginning water training
4. Working from the shore
5. Multiple boats

Evidence-Search Training

1. Qualify in wilderness training
2. Mechanics of the alert
3. Beginning article
4. Hidden article

Small-Area or Fine Search Techniques

1. Qualify in wilderness training
2. Evidence search (no retrieve)
3. Fine search techniques

Cadaver Training

1. Qualify in wilderness training
2. Introduce the scent
3. Teach the alert
4. Search for the scent
5. Above-ground cadaver
6. Underground cadaver

7. Fine search techniques
8. Proof the dog

Avalanche Training

1. Qualify in wilderness training
2. Preparing for avalanche training
3. Finding a missing person

Disaster Training

1. Qualify for airscent training
2. Obedience
3. Additional commands
4. Buried assistant
5. Live bodies only (*if this is what the handler wants*)
6. Advanced disaster work
7. Mass-fatality search training

APPENDIX B:
SAR DOG HANDLER TRAINING

Different regions of the country have different search circumstances and types of terrain that require specific training. Another factor in training is the types of mission that the unit is called to assist on. Listed below are some of the required areas of training, as well as additional training that the SAR dog handler will need. In many cases, taking a course in another discipline will help a SAR dog handler understand the needs of the mission, even if the handler is not qualified to perform that type of operation.

If you are not sure what type of training to get, consult with local units, park rangers, fire departments, or emergency services. I feel that the starred items are a minimum requirement for SAR dog handlers.

* First Aid—Minimum Red Cross First Aid Training, including CPR
* Managing the Search Operation or Managing the Search Function
* Visual Mantracking (*done by the handler, not the dog*)
* Orienteering/Map and Compass/ Topographical Map Reading, GPS Navigation
* Unstable Structure Awareness
* Canine First Aid
* Management of Spontaneous Volunteers
* Helicopter Operations for SAR
* Personal Preparedness for SAR
* Wilderness Survival
* Water Self-Rescue
* Critical Incident Stress Management (*to know at least what it is and when to use it*)
* Crime Scene Preservation for Both Live and Cadaver Searching
• Hazardous Materials (HAZMAT) Training
• Emergency Medical Technician
• Wilderness Medical Training

• Urban Medicine
• Avalanche Survival Training
• Heavy Rescue
• High Angle Rescue
• Confined Space Rescue
• Ocean Rescue Techniques
• Swift Water Rescue
• Beach and Surf Rescue
• Trauma of the Elderly
• Pediatric Trauma
• Trauma Care in the Field
• In-Water Helicopter Rescue
• Canine Rope Rescue Techniques
• Infrared Resources
• Nutrition and Fluid Replacement for SAR
• Resource Status Display System
• Field Electronics Navigation Techniques
• Geographic Information Systems for Emergency Response
• Urban SAR Problems
• Mountain Rescue Techniques and Survival
• Desert Survival

APPENDIX C:
RESOURCES

At the first writing of this book, the Internet was not available for research. Today, the reader can search online for many SAR resources. However, to help the reader, certain Web sites, books, and other publications are listed here.

Web Site

National Search Dog Alliance: www.n-sda.org

Books

Bauer, Nona Kilgore. *Dog Heroes of September 11th: A Tribute to America's Search and Rescue Dogs.* Allenhurst, NJ: Kennel Club Books, 2006.

Bryson, Sandy. *Search Dog Training.* Pacific Grove, CA: The Boxwood Press, 1984.

Bulanda, Susan. *Ready to Serve, Ready To Save: Strategies of Real-Life Search and Rescue Missions.* Wilsonville, OR: Doral Publishing, 1994.

Bulanda, Susan. *Scenting on the Wind: Scent Work for Hunting Dogs.* Sun City, AZ: Doral Publishing, 2002.

Burnett, Patti. *Avalanche! Hasty Search, The Care and Training of Avalanche Search and Rescue Dogs.* Phoenix, AZ: Doral Publishing, 2003.

Button, Lue. *Practical Scent Dog Training.* Loveland, CO: Alpine Publications, 1990.

Gorny, Boguslaw P. *Tracking for Search and Rescue Dogs: A Practical Manual for Novice and Advanced Handlers.* Calgary, Alberta, Canada: Detselig Enterprises, Ltd., 2003.

Hammond, Shirley M. *Training the Disaster Search Dog.* Wenatchee, WA: Dogwise, 2006.

Johnson, Glen R. *Tracking Dog Theory & Methods.* Rome, NY: Arner Publications, 1977.

Koester, Robert J. *Lost Person Behavior.* Charlottesville, VA: dbS Productions, 2008.

LaValla, Patrick "Rick," *Search is an Emergency.* Olympia, WA: ERI International, Inc., 1999.

Pearsall, Milo D. and Hugo Verbruggen, MD. *Scent: Training to Track, Search and Rescue.* Loveland, CO: Alpine Publications, 1982.

Preston, Lisa, *Canine Scent Work Log.* Crawford, CO: Alpine Publications, 2007.

Rebmann, Andrew, Edward David, and Marcella H. Sorg. *Cadaver Dog Handbook: Forensic Training and Tactics for the Recovery of Human Remains.* Boca Raton, FL: CRC Press, 2000.

Tolhurst, William, D. *Manhunters! Hounds of the Big T.* Puyallup, WA: Hound Dog Press, 1984.

Tweedie, Jan. *On The Trail! A Practical Guide to the Working Bloodhound and Other Search and Rescue Dogs.* Loveland, CO: Alpine Publications, 1998.

Supplies

Sigma-Aldrich canine cadaver training scents:
PO Box 14508
St. Louis, MO 63178
800-325-3010
www.sigmaaldrich.com

SoftTech™ cadaver parts, part of the Techline Trauma Moulage and Appendages line:
Techline Technologies, Inc.
668 Davisville Road
Willow Grove, PA 19090
David Parry, Jr., 215-657-1909 or
David.Parry2@mpstechline.com
www.techlinetrauma.com and
www.techlinerocks.com

INDEX

CPSIA information can be obtained
at www.ICGtesting.com
Printed in the USA
LVOW01s0958010317
525732LV00003B/6/P